You're It!

Successful Single Mothering After Divorce

Jeanne L. Ward

Eloquent Books

Eloquent Books
An imprint of Strategic Book Group
P.O. Box 333
Durham CT 06422
www.StrategicBookGroup.com

Library of Congress Control Number: 2010932319

ISBN: 978-1-60911-465-7

Printed in the United States of America

Book Design: Stacie Tingen

Dedication

For my daughters, Barbara and Laura, who lived this journey with me as children and have grown into amazing women.

For my beloved husband, Charlie.

For my sons-in-law, Mark D. and Mark B. – good men.

For our grandchildren: Lawton Brantley, Holland Anne, Harrison Bradley, Sophie Grace, Max Benjamin, and Eva Ward, who fill our lives with joy and wonder and are our link to and hope for the future.

Table of Contents

Introduction

I remember the day I fully realized I was indeed a single mother. A friend and I had taken our children to the beach for the night so that my husband could move out without all of us there watching our life being disassembled. I'll always be glad I was not around when he took his pipe and pipe stand, his favorite chair, his saxophone and record collection, the framed Hippocratic Oath which I gave him when he graduated from medical school, and all the other things, large and small, which defined our life together. Since we had been together since high school, there was a lot of "us" stuff.

We returned from the beach in the early evening. The house was dark and, when I opened the door, it had an eerie stillness, as if life had been sucked out of it; actually, it had. The life we had made in this, our first home, was gone, just as his possessions, books, and clothes were gone. Fortunately, the girls were tired from the sun and beach and had fallen asleep in the car, so I carefully carried them to bed and tucked them in.

The spots vacant of Dad's things would be glaringly obvious in the morning light, as would the reality of his absence, but tonight it was quiet and dark. He often took all-night call at the hospital, so I was used to him not being there, but tonight felt different and, of course, it was. It was the beginning of our life as a threesome and mine as a single mother.

Many years have passed since that night, and my daughters, in their thirties, are wives and mothers raising a group of six amazing little people. They are caring, good women, who bring me more joy than they will ever know.

It has always been in the back of my mind to write this book, but a conversation at a luncheon with a newly divorced young woman gave me the impetus to get this done. She was a recently divorced mother of three young girls and she expressed her concerns about how they could grow up well-adjusted, when all she read was how many problems children of divorce experienced. The whole tone of her conversation was of a woman who believed she was defeated before she even started.

Suddenly, it became clear to me that I must write this book to let single mothers struggling with too many responsibilities and too little time know that the children they raise can turn into well-adjusted adults, capable of forming healthy relationships, respecting – not blaming – mom, and finding their own place in the world. I wanted to help single mothers believe in themselves and their children.

During my years as a counselor, I have worked a great deal with single fathers' groups. I have also, through my single parenting classes, got to know and respect many single fathers and their perspectives. But, there are very subtle and sometimes not so subtle differences in the way single mothers and fathers are perceived and, therefore, treated in society.

My favorite illustration is "the ponytail test." During one of my single parenting classes we devised a test: one mother and one father in the class would send their daughters (ages six and seven) to school with a crooked ponytail and three buttons missing somewhere on their clothes. We all waited for the report the following week. The little girl of the father returned home from school with her ponytail redone correctly and a note from the teacher that she knew how hard it was for a man to do "these things," so if he sent in the buttons she would be glad to help. The little girl of the mother, on the other hand, returned home with her same crooked ponytail from the morning and no offer of help with buttons.

As a former school counselor, it's easy for me to imagine the conversation in the teachers' lounge. Teachers would be muttering about the poor single father doing his best, while the discussion about the single mother would be how awful it was that *she* let her daughter come to school like that; probably out until all hours. Single fathers have hero status, while single mothers are the gay divorcees! The ponytail test was sadly revealing. As a result, all the women in the class – myself included – took advanced ponytail lessons, lest we be judged so harshly.

This book is by no means intended to take away from the notion that family life is at its ideal state when children have two caring, involved parents. Single mothers are the first to celebrate the ideal, but they are living a different reality. No new mother gazes at her newborn in the nursery and looks forward to raising the child alone. I know I certainly didn't! It does not take a genius to realize that when one person does what two people were going to do, it requires a great deal of work and altered expectations. But, knowing that you can succeed makes all the difference. And, trust me, you can.

When I divorced in the late 1970s, gloom and doom surrounded single parents, particularly single mothers. Families of those who were divorced were referred to as "broken families." The term was never used to describe a widowed woman's family. I remember one Sunday morning, not long after my divorce, my seven-year-old leaned over and asked me after the sermon if we were a real family or a broken one. The question saddened me. A lifelong Catholic, educated entirely in Catholic schools, the attitude in that church did *not* represent the religion that I knew. Then I got angry, really angry, and a chance encounter with the new bishop in our diocese gave me a positive way to channel that anger. The next year, working with this caring bishop, we founded the first ministry in our diocese for divorced Catholics, which I headed for five years. I'm happy to say still exists today.

People have always been benevolent toward the widows: brought them food, helped with the children. But a divorced mother was a different story. Believe me, there were days, actually quite a few, when a big bowl of mashed potatoes, the ultimate comfort food, would have been a delicacy.

But by some unwritten rule, divorced mothers are not on the casserole circuit. Never mind that your husband may have been abusive or run off with a Cindy Crawford look-a-like; there was an unspoken notion that a real woman could keep her family together.

One person can raise a family, but it takes two people to make a marriage. No one truly understands what lies at the heart of a marriage. As John Taylor writes in his personal account of his own divorce in his deeply insightful book, *Falling*, "No one I knew who has decided to divorce undertook it lightly. It was a wrenching decision, fraught with remorse and heartache, imperiled by moments of genuine terror, and it had almost inevitably been postponed for years. Who had the right, I wanted to know, to moralize about these choices, to add the weight of public censure to the private anguish they already entailed?"

There was also the notion held by many of those who were unhappily married that, as a divorced woman, you were having a wicked, exciting, and independent life. I remember one evening returning late from work, lugging milk, pet food, and cheerios, about to face the babysitter, dinner, homework, wash, and oh yes, two small girls eager for my attention. One was crying because our pet gerbil looked sick; the other said her stomach hurt. Around the corner of the house appeared my married neighbor, and she said that it must be nice to be alone and do what I wanted. My mouth fell open at the stupidity of her comment and only years of training by the nuns kept me from killing her with a gallon of milk. Do what I wanted? *When?* I couldn't remember the last time I did what I wanted! I have a close friend who says she really never considered herself "single" until her children were grown.

Another widely-held misconception today is that being a single mother must be easier since, in the last thirty years, so many women head households and divorce is so common. It is true that when I, at the age of thirty, became a single mother, I did not know anyone my age who was divorced with children, particularly in the Catholic culture that I inhabited. Community resources, employer awareness of family issues, and flexible child-care were non-existent. Today our society is very aware and concerned about mothers and the children they are raising. In some ways, they are too concerned. Single mothers are now blamed for everything wrong in our society, from delinquent children, poor school performance, to violent behavior, lack of respect for authority, probably global warming as well. When children of a mother alone commit crimes, the media frenzy focuses on these poor, latchkey, unloved children, raised by an irresponsible, careless mother. No one seemed to know what to say when the nation discovered that the most brutal school killing of our century, at Columbine, was committed by two boys both from two-parent families.

These attitudes make it hard for single mothers to believe they can succeed. A little less societal concern might be better. For all these reasons, at the end of the day, I must write about that which I know best and feel in my heart and soul: the experience of a single, divorced mother.

When I think of what it means to be a single mother, I recall in vivid detail a night when my older daughter was eight and her sister five. I came home from work to discover that the eight-year-old had spiked a high fever very quickly, and it continued to climb. I called our pediatrician (more about this *very* important person in your life later) who listened, and then in a calm voice told me to put her immediately in the car and take her to the emergency room; he would meet us there. He did not want to alarm me, but he did *not* like the intensity and speed of her illness.

I will never forget that ride to the hospital, with a frightened five-year-old in the back seat, and the very sick little girl with her head in my lap. It wouldn't have mattered that night if someone told me that half the known world was made up of single mothers; it would have been no comfort. I was alone, really alone, rushing through the night with no other adult to reassure me.

For a single mother, when you lock the door at night, it is like the games of childhood where you get tapped on the shoulder and someone says, "You're it." This book is about what to do when *you're it!*

About the Author

Jeanne L. Ward brings together a variety of professional and personal experiences to create *You're It! Successful Single Mothering After Divorce.* With a B.A. in Elementary Education and an M.A. in Counseling Psychology, Mrs. Ward worked as an elementary school teacher and later as a school counselor. In this role, she started groups for children of divorce. The notes from these groups form the basis of this book. As an adjunct professor for the local community college, she authored and taught the courses "Divorce: A New Challenge" and "Single Parenting – Becoming a New Kind of Family," along with other courses relating to work and family.

Her professional career also includes high-profile jobs in legislative affairs, lobbying for four local mayors, and serving as an economic development consultant in the private sector. Mrs. Ward's work with the media includes serving as an editorial writer for the local *Post-Newsweek Station.* In addition, through her column, "Relatively Speaking," she shared many articles about family life in the *Florida Times-Union.* She currently co-hosts a local political talk show, *First Coast Views,* and has participated in many speaking engagements about work and family issues.

As a community volunteer, Mrs. Ward founded the Ministry for Divorced Catholics in the local diocese and served as its director for five years. With friend and child development expert, Lenora Gregory, she founded the non-profit organization, Family Care Connections, which endeavors to influence corporate entities to implement family-friendly policies. For twenty years, this organization has honored local businesses through the Week of the Working Parent. Mrs. Ward's current community activities include Chairman of Hope Haven Children's and Family Clinic and board membership for Jacksonville International Airport Arts Commission and Dignity-You-Wear.

Mrs. Ward has been recognized for her contributions through numerous awards over the years, including the *Florida Times-Union* "Eve Award," the National Council of Jewish Women's "Women of Power Award," "Advocate of the Year" from the People with AIDS Coalition, and poster honoree for the Mayor's Commission for the Status of Women, among others.

The greatest motivation in writing this book for single mothers after divorce was her own personal experience as a single mother of two small daughters. She now resides in Jacksonville, Florida, with her husband, Charlie.

Chapter One

You're It! Will the Real Adult Please Stand Up?

We all know a single mother like this: She and her children are buddies. They dress alike, share adventures and giggles about their dates, and live like roommates, with everyone having an opinion and no one making a decision. This book is about how to move beyond the "children as roommates" mentality and become a mother in charge.

Ordinarily, when the reality sets in that you really are "it," the normal response is to get into bed and pull the covers over your head, and comfort yourself with chocolate chip cookies. I have a personal theory that there is no life crisis not made a bit more bearable by chocolate in some form. Once you have eaten all the chocolate chip cookies you can stand and the crumbs are driving you from the bed, take an honest look at yourself and see which of the following syndromes you might have (it may be a combination), and begin the real work of becoming a responsible single mother. By the way, along the road of life, a day in bed with cookies is allowed from time to time.

The Rose Garden Syndrome

A wonderful friend of mine, now deceased, gave life to the Rose Garden Syndrome. She was in a graduate school class and a student commented on the plight of working women raising children alone. The professor came back with, "Well, no one ever promised you a rose garden!"

My friend stood, calling upon the warm, southern accent she acquired growing up in a small Georgia town, and said, "Well, I do declare, everyone *did* promise me a rose garden. If I was a good girl and did everything right, things would work out. They lied."

She had married young and had three boys. When they were five, six, and eight, her husband left her for someone else. She was never able to get past how unfair it all was. She had never pictured herself in any role but homemaker, despite the fact that she was a gifted speaker and writer.

She refused to work from an office and mostly worked on her bed, developing seminars. Somehow, her being home made all the changes seem less real. Everyone around her was aware of this "unfair thing," especially her children.

The truth is that we did not discover the world was unfair when we were divorced, but much earlier. I discovered it when I was eight and had my *third* baby brother and not a sister. Or maybe the day in second grade when the boy in back of me was pulling my hair and I got in trouble for yelling at him. We have always known about *unfair*, not just from the magnitude of divorce. In the world of unfair, this is *major*, as my children used to say.

If you are prone to overindulging in self-pity, try something that I used in my divorce adjustment classes. The class was three hours long and the potential for hours of blood-curdling divorce horrors was plentiful. To counter this, for the first fifteen minutes of class, everyone could wallow in self-pity as much as they liked. They were free to bring wedding pictures, describe the perfect (young) body of the wife who replaced them, and on and on. You get the idea: basically a group wallow. But, at the end of fifteen minutes, the wallow was over and for the next two hours and forty-five minutes, we worked on the future.

Maybe a good wallow before you start the day will get it behind you. Motivate yourself by thinking about how little you like being around people who feel sorry for themselves: poor helpless victims in a cruel world. You don't want to become that bitter person and you surely don't want to raise your children to be like that. At the end of the six-month divorce class, the wallow time was almost non-existent. Remember, you are not a victim of divorce. You are a woman who has had a divorce as a part of her life experience: *big* difference.

The Popularity Contest Syndrome

No young girl growing up in America is untouched by the September ritual of Miss America. If you could not be Miss America, the next best thing to be was Miss Congeniality: the one everyone likes. Now, give this some thought. How sweet must you be to get forty-nine women to vote for you? Clearly, you couldn't have told anyone that her song was off-key or her swimsuit a bit snug. You couldn't have had a grumpy day during competition or yelled at anyone because she took your hairdryer. In other words, the way to get this award was for everyone to like you. Motherhood, and certainly not single motherhood, is not a popularity contest.

Some of the things that mothers need to do, and *must do*, will not help you win a popularity contest, but will help your children become mature and happy adults. Many women want to turn away from the role of the mother who makes hard decisions; some even fall quickly into re-marriage so they don't have to face these decisions alone.

Re-marriage is not a solution for this. Think for a minute, why would some poor man feel honored to take the role of enforcer with your children, when you don't want to do it? Unless he's never been married and has been living with his mother (a book in itself), he probably faces the same children issues you do.

The sooner you accept the fact that to be a good mother you can't be popular all the time, the happier you will be. Unfortunately the period surrounding a divorce is not a particularly self-esteem building, feel-good time, so it is especially hard to hear even an unkind word from your children. A possible motivator is to close your eyes and picture the worst behaved child you have ever known (we all remember one). See him or her at six, ten, fourteen, eighteen. Now open your eyes and take charge. No one wants to live with that! This imaginary child's behavior was probably sort of cute at six, wearing thin at fourteen, and downright scary by eighteen.

The Family as a Committee Syndrome

We all know that old joke that men tell about how they are in charge of all the big things in the family like world peace, global warming, and terrorism, and the wife is in charge of the little things like where they live, what car they drive, and where the children go to school. This humorous vignette seems quaint today. Many people advocate the democratic approach to family life, like "teams" in corporate America where decisions are made as a group. Many single mothers get confused about this and how their "committee" should function. First of all, unless you have only one child, you are always outnumbered. Second, as a single mother, you must decide where you live, what school your children attend, who takes care of them when you are working, and other major matters. Only *you* possess the knowledge and ability to make these things happen. Children don't make these decisions in two-parent families. Why should they in a single-parent family?

When there are areas that children can appropriately make decisions themselves, they should. For example, letting them pick a fast food restaurant they like or wearing what clothes they want (this one may spark controversy, but remember, no one ever went to first grade in their pajamas).

They can decide which friends to have over. The list grows and changes as your children do. Decisions, even unpopular ones like moving, which often occurs after a divorce, are yours to make. And you don't have to defend them. Let the children stick to the pizza places and what clothes to wear. Like the quaint joke, you make the big *and* little decisions, but I doubt you have much time to devote to global warming!

The Queen for a Day Syndrome

There was a show in the early days of TV called *Queen for a Day*. As a child, I was fascinated by it, and even at a young age was confused by the premise upon which the show was built. Women came on and told about the hardships of their lives: house fires, abandonment, illnesses, etc. The audience would vote, and the woman with the worst problem was crowned "Queen for a Day." She actually got a crown and was showered with such gifts as a washing machine, clothes, food, and children's toys. I never did understand how a new washing machine would make all those terrible things better.

In reality, the Queen was getting emotional and financial rewards for being a victim. The show no longer exists, thank goodness, but unfortunately, women who like to play the role of victim still do. In this syndrome, you think of yourself as the victim of cruel people and events. Even if this is true, pull away from the dangerous role of a woman who refuses to take charge, and change what you can change. The very first thing you can and should change is your own attitude. You will discover over time that you will start to feel better about yourself, and more confident as your attitude improves. Take charge and let your children know that you are there as a mom and will take care of them. All the Queens for a Day in the world let their children flounder as they wait to be rescued by the king. And, even if the king does appear, he probably has a kingdom to run and children to raise, and wouldn't be interested in a victim as his queen!

Before you go to the rest of the book, read and re-read this chapter.

To Become – An Adult Woman

1. When you no longer act like a victim, you will no longer feel like a victim.
2. Accept the unfairness of the situation, and then lay it to rest.
3. Embrace the role of mother-in-charge.
4. Remember that mothers are always loved, and only sometimes liked.

Chapter Two

The Man that I Married: Letting Go and Moving On

There is a part of the wedding ceremony where the minister asks the congregation, "If anyone knows why this couple should not be joined in holy matrimony, let them speak now or forever hold their peace." At my first wedding, no one jumped to their feet and proclaimed deep, dark secrets about either of us that brought the ceremony to an abrupt end. But when people heard that we were divorcing more than a decade later, everyone had an opinion and apparently my husband had Charles Manson qualities that I never noticed. Usually, this information is shared in the following way: your mother's long time friend and church circle member (who gave you a kitchen shower) pulls you aside at the grocery store and whispers that she's so sorry about the "situation" but she always had a "bad feeling" about him. Then she proceeds to pat your hand and call you a "poor dear."

This scene is repeated with a number of creative variations, but the message is the same in all of them. First, you were stupid and picked the wrong person to marry and father your children. Second, you have somehow gone from being a wife and mother to a "poor dear."

I wonder if these people realize that if they had jumped to their feet at my wedding and shared their insight, they might have saved me a lot of trouble. Apparently the fact that I have been married to this person for years is nothing compared to their instincts. For many people (with too much time on their hands), a divorce is a time to assign blame like, "She spent all her time at work," or "He went out a lot at night with the boys."

Everyone, no matter how removed from your life, has an opinion. But at the end of the day, no one has to live it out except you, your husband, and your children, as you all face the painful end of your marriage. While gossipy details may serve to bring a bit of excitement and intrigue to other people's lives, it is extremely unhealthy and not in the best interest of you or your children to buy into it.

During the turmoil of a divorce, there is always a moment when we think that if we could go back in time with our current knowledge, we would make different choices. In the movie *Peggy Sue Got Married*, Kathleen Turner as Peggy Sue gets to do what many of us fantasize about at one time or another: go back in time with the knowledge that we have now. But alas, Peggy Sue goes back, and given the circumstances at the time, she makes the same choices that she did originally.

Go back to a time before children and try to recapture the feelings that led you to marry, plan a life, and have children together. Whatever happened later, for a moment in time, however brief, you both had hopes and dreams for a future together. No one could look into the years ahead and see that those hopes and dreams would never be fulfilled, no matter what your mother's friend says or any other psychic relatives who feel the need to analyze your divorce. I've seen people, myself included, marry people with similar backgrounds, goals, religion, race, education, and childhood friends, and still end up divorced, while other people with apparently nothing in common and a short courtship end up celebrating their 50th anniversaries. Despite all we know about relationships today (from Dr. Ruth to Dr. Phil), there is still mystery about the bonds that connect couples that enable them to stay together and grow as people while creating a life together. It is some combination of luck, love, and commitment. The exact balance is hard to find and keep.

I recently came across a picture taken about a year before my divorce. It is at my daughter's fourth birthday party; it shows smiling children, me cutting the cake, and my husband to the side, removed and distant. How did I not see it at the time? He was there for the cake and the picture, but he was emotionally gone. He was never Charles Manson. He was just a young husband who had already moved past us to another life.

If we are honest, really honest, with ourselves as women, then the hardest part of divorce is the loss of our hopes and dreams for a family together. You often hear about people divorcing shortly after a new baby comes or a new home is finished, and you wonder why they went ahead and did these things. The baby and the house are desperate attempts by two people to convince themselves that their hopes and dreams are still alive.

In my divorce adjustment classes, I frequently asked women who were mourning their divorce and wishing things were "the way they used to be" to describe exactly what they missed the most. Often they mourned the lifestyle, the safety of being a couple, the security of a partner in parenting, but not the man himself.

For women who mourned the loss of the husband, lover, companion, or the man himself, the divorce adjustment is much harder. For them, it is the loss of a deep love and not just a lifestyle. In the end, the women all wanted to live out the marriage they had planned when they were young and for their husband to be the prince they had envisioned.

As we discussed in the first chapter, in the Rose Garden Syndrome, some of us believe that we deserve to have it all work out like Cinderella. Let's think about this. All we know about the prince in Cinderella is that he was good looking and had a great horse. We'll never know if he was from a dysfunctional family or if he had problems with intimacy. Remember that they only met once: at a ball, for heaven's sake! But we do know that Cinderella suffered at the hands of the wicked stepmother and two stepsisters, probably the most evil and unattractive trio ever to inhabit a fairy tale. So Cinderella, by virtue of all these trials, deserved the good looking prince on the great horse and all future happiness. Other than that, all we know about her is that she had tiny feet. Too bad we can't revisit the prince and Cinderella on their 10th anniversary.

If you have not conquered the Rose Garden Syndrome, then you are in real danger of coming down with the chronic and fatal disease of single mothers: bitterness. Unfortunately, no shot can prevent this disease, just hard work and a willingness to look back at your marriage, extract the good, forgive yourself and your spouse for the painful loss of dreams, and move on.

Divorce can change a lot of things about your life: your economic status, where you live, the number of presents under the Christmas tree. But, it cannot – I repeat, cannot – change you into a bitter person unless you let it. Bitterness doesn't just appear like a rash; it is nurtured by days and years of dwelling on the bad, unfair, evil things done to you, going over them until you lose all perspective about yourself and others. Every one of us can think of a woman like this. She's unhappy, bitter, alone, and never has a kind word for anyone. She has a chip on her shoulder. She wonders why her children don't like to visit (after all, she *did* raise them alone, after their no-good father left). You do not want to become this person, for your sake and the sake of your children. Be conscious of the symptoms of this disease, excessive self-pity and sarcasm, as well as the belief that "everyone is happy but me."

If you have any or all of these symptoms, run, don't walk, to your nearest mental health clinic, find someone to talk to, and work this through. This is the greatest challenge of a divorced mother, to take whatever happened and work through it until you make peace with it. There are terrible things that people do to each other, particularly when a private life is thrust into the legal system, and the outcomes are often cruel and unfair. No matter what the result, resolve not to let it harden your heart and soul. In truth, how you come to grips with the end of your marriage and the new relationship with your former husband will determine, to a great extent, how well you emerge as a person and how well adjusted your children will be under your care.

No matter what has happened in your marriage or after, this man will forever be the father of your children. I am very fortunate to have a kind and caring second husband who has assumed the day-to-day role of father, shopping with my girls for prom dresses, walking them down the aisle at their weddings, and everything in between and beyond. But rejection is a powerful thing and even in their absence, fathers cast a shadow over children's lives. In absence, there is longing.

On your worst days, when you are in a Queen for a Day mode and you are wallowing in victimization, awash in chocolate chip cookies, it might make you feel better to think of your former spouse as Charles Manson and you as a saintly victim. Think about this: on no day is it comforting for a child to think of their father as Charles Manson, because they are linked to this person by genetics, heredity, and destiny. You, on the other hand, are linked only by choice and a contract that can be undone. Your children need to come to know their father, good and bad, on their own, not through your filter of the hurt and pain of a failed marriage. This is why it is so important to recall the good times of their baby years to give them some joy, however brief, in terms of their parents' marriage.

There is another picture that I found recently, and I was struck by the hopeful, young faces looking back at me. It is in a hospital room the day after my oldest daughter was born. I am holding her awkwardly and my husband is sitting nervously on the edge of the bed. We are looking with awe and amazement at our new daughter. The three of us are frozen in time: young and hopeful. Hold on to that moment, forgive each other for lost dreams, and pass on the hope to your children. They are the living proof of the good that was.

To Become – Formerly Married

1. Divorce cannot make you a bitter person. Only you can do that.
2. You are no longer a wife, but your former spouse will forever be a father.
3. Forgive your spouse and let go – really let go.
4. Invent your future and don't live in your past.

Chapter Three

Sunday, Sunday: Parenting after Divorce

When people are trying to describe the depths of their feelings for their children, trying to impress you with how much they love them, they frequently say how they would, without a second thought, throw themselves in front of a train to save them. Who can argue with such courage and self-sacrifice? I, for one, contend that this is a whole lot less impressive than it appears at first glance. In fact, I think it's the coward's way out. If you throw yourself in front of a train to save little Oscar, you die a hero. In addition, you don't have to stay around to do homework, enforce rules, drive five million carpools, prepare countless cupcakes, and recite to little Oscar the most famous line in all of parenting: "I don't care if everyone else in the world is doing it. If everyone was jumping off a bridge, would you too?" Certainly a lot less glamorous than the train option.

Parenting is by its very nature a personal commitment to the physical and emotional well-being of a child grounded by unconditional love. Rarely is parenthood played out in the dramatic train scenario, but rather in the small, daily rituals of children and parents: meal time, bedtime stories, talking about a new friend at school, a hard lesson in sharing, a sun-drenched day at the beach, planning the ever-important birthday party, a new baby, a warm hug, and so many more too numerous to mention. Whether it is preparing for the tooth fairy or picking a wedding dress, this is the stuff that nurtures and feeds the parent-child relationship. Some days this commitment is as easy as a small child seeking comfort in our touch, or as hard as holding your own with a defiant teenager forging their own path. The basic core of parenthood is the same if you are married or divorced, and the same rituals and challenges face us as we help our children grow.

There is no question, however, that single parenting presents some unique challenges; some small, some large. Small is like remembering to buy milk before you come home, because if you forget, then all of you, pajama-clad baby and all, will have to make that trip to the store since you are the only adult in the house. Large is accepting the fact that the only person whose parenting style you control is you. Small you will catch onto very quickly, since it doesn't take too many ventures into the night with sleepy little ones to make you remember the milk. Large will take longer to understand and implement, but no concept is more crucial to your success as a single parent.

Once the reality sets in that you are alone with your children, the door is locked for the night, and you've eaten a box of chocolate chip cookies in bed (one of *those* days), it is important to look at your new parenting role. Think about it in light of how you have functioned as a parent in your marriage and how you want to go forward as a parent. It is really an opportunity to take a hard look at your parenting style and figure out what you expect of yourself and your children. This requires taking a long look at your parenting style as a couple and how you need to change to adapt to your new status. For example, if you left the discipline to your husband and were the *fun* mom, then you are familiar with the phrase, "Just wait until your dad comes home." You need to think about discipline and how you want to approach it. If, however, you were the parent who set the rules and enforced them, and your spouse had the *fun* role, then you need to figure out how to be firm and fun.

In my divorce and single parenting classes, I often heard people panic at the thought of parenting alone. Yet, when they thought about it honestly, they realized that they had been parenting alone for a long time, with the illusion of a supportive spouse. Perhaps you will realize that you and your spouse never did develop a parenting style. Whatever the former situation, now is the time for you to become a mother-in-charge and develop your own style.

The easiest way to map out your parenting strategy is to think seriously about the values you want your child to have as an adult and then create an environment that reinforces these values. Create a *few* rules that are consistent with those values. For example, you may decide that you want your child to be:

1. an honest person
2. a person respectful of others' feelings and possessions
3. a person responsible with their school work

Once you have established your position, then do three crucial things:

1. Reserve your strongest reactions and consequences for violations of these values.
2. Reinforce the positive things your child does with these values.
3. Do *not* get sidetracked by small, less important issues.

This may sound overly simple, but in fact it works because it is simple. You look at the big picture of parenting, pick out the essential values and then reinforce them for the next eighteen years. It really is a parenting plan

You frequently hear people in speeches and graduation addresses talk about the core values they learned at home – honesty, kindness, industriousness – and the way these values have stayed with them. This is because every day was reinforcement in some way of these values, while less important behavior was ignored.

My daughter had a friend in grade school who told her that she could never figure out what was important to do because her parents got equally as furious if she spilled juice as they did when she told a lie. If you want your child to equate a clumsy lurch at the orange juice with a deceitful act, then scream on. As parents, we get sidetracked by less important issues. The best example is the clean bedroom scenario. Perfectly rational parents have been known to abandon all notions of an honest polite, studious child to have a child who keeps a clean room. My father was a child psychiatrist and he never told parents that a clean room was a predictor of future emotional health and success. In fact, growing up, our rooms were ours to do with as we liked. There were a few rules: when the room was messy the door needed to be closed, and a path had to exist from the bed to the door in case of an emergency. One of my three brothers had a room where no one ever went because it was such a wreck. I'm sure my mother ventured in from time to time, but I really can't recall many forays there myself. His door was closed most of the time, and despite that, he grew into a fine, professional man with, yes, a very neat house. I do, however, remember the thunderous reaction and punishment for lies. As a result, in adulthood, I value a clean bedroom little and honesty greatly. Think hard about what you want your children to value in the future, then act accordingly.

The same principle applied to the firestorm over long hair on boys in the 1960s, and the equally fierce adult reaction to tattoos and pierced body parts today. In fact, for a number of years, as a school counselor, I worked with delinquent boys who told me that their parents got so distracted yelling about their appearance that they could get away with drinking and drugs, serious offenses that went unnoticed in the parental quest for a good look over a good act.

Parenting is a matter of picking your battles. A purple tattoo may annoy you, but a cruel child will devastate you. Put your energy and strongest reactions where your values are, and reinforce good behavior at every opportunity. This does not mean that you don't get angry and frustrated about lesser offenses, but it does mean that you need to have a clear agenda of what you expect of your children, and they need to know it.

Now that you have developed your strategy and are ready to move forward as the mother-in-charge, it is time to return to a crucial concept introduced early in this chapter: *the only person whose parenting you can control is you.* You cannot preach, suggest, or control the parenting style that your former spouse will adopt. Your suggestions will not be well-received: accept the fact that your children's father may operate from a different set of values, and perhaps that is one of the reasons you are no longer married. As long as your children are in no physical or emotional danger – in which case you would need to act *at once* to protect them – you cannot control the parenting in their father's house. Oh, and by the way, abuse and neglect is not:

1. eating a Happy Meal three times a day
2. going to bed without a bath
3. wearing clothes to bed instead of pajamas
4. staying up late

Remember, these things are not abuse or neglect, and time and attention for your children from their father is important, however unconventionally given. Women often complain after a child has been with the father that they need to "undo" all the damage of a weekend of lax discipline. Were the weekend's activities really inappropriate, or are you objecting because you are not in control? Or worse yet, are you letting old anger at your spouse emerge? Keep focused on your tasks as a parent and stop worrying about what he's doing. Remember, no one ever died from wearing their clothes to bed.

For most divorced families, Sunday night is a particularly difficult time. It is painfully clear that our children live in two separate families when they return home on Sunday night, still caught up in where they were with Dad, adjusting to where they are with Mom. As single mothers greeting returning children, make Sunday night as low key and calm as possible.

Do not:

1. have a group of people there when they return home and expect them to blend in
2. ask them a million questions and then criticize what you hear
3. make disparaging remarks about their appearance
4. criticize their father

Just listen and comfort them if they are sad about the transition. Give them a little space and time to re-adjust, sound enthused if they had a good time, and leave it at that. This whole process will not go well if you have not come to grips with your feelings about your spouse, as discussed in the last chapter. Keep working through those negative feelings. Get help, pray, talk to a trusted friend, but keep at it until you get it right. Nothing is harder or more important. You owe it to yourself and your children.

The full realization of what divorce means is captured in the Sunday night ritual of returning children. For a father, there is pain in returning to a place he used to call home. For a mother, there is pain in seeing her former spouse leave and assuming all the responsibility again. So on Sunday night, shut the door, have ice cream and cookies with your children, and call it a day: Sunday.

To Become – A Mother Who Parents Alone

1. Commit yourself to the physical and emotional well-being of your children.
2. Repeat to yourself daily, "The only person whose parenting I control is me."
3. Pick the values you want your child to have and reinforce them.
4. Remember, as long as your child is safe, the parenting style of their father is not yours to judge.

Chapter Four

Your House or Mine? Children as Power Brokers

One of the most revealing and thought provoking sessions with the children's group started with seven-year-old Amy telling everyone that she was always forgetting things as she went from her father's house on Monday, Tuesday, and Wednesday, and to her mother's on Thursday, Friday, and Saturday, with Sunday split each week. That day, she had left her good sweater at her dad's and her mom was angry with her. Amy said, "Nobody is ever happy with me." Listening to her schedule, I don't think I would ever have two shoes that matched in the same house. Amy was clearly overwhelmed and her friends shared similar frustrating experiences.

Suddenly, Kevin, age eight, who had been listening but was not talking, rose to his feet and announced that he knew how to get Mom and Dad to do what he wanted. In the manner of an old sage giving advice to the masses (in this case wide-eyed children), he said, "If your mom is mad at you, tell her that you want to live with Dad. If Dad is mad at you, tell him you don't like his girlfriend and don't want to visit anymore."

Some people will say that an eight-year-old child would not be capable of such strategy or manipulation. But let us not forget that these children are fighting with all they have to hold on to the one thing they know – their family together. Never underestimate what anyone will do to keep what matters most to them, and children are no exception. Have you ever played the game of Concentration with a child? They are completely focused and they always win. They play with single-minded concentration while we adults are thinking about deadlines and unfinished tasks. That same focus and concentration is aimed at keeping their parents together.

Over the years, I had heard parents say that they fought all the time, so, "Didn't the children realize we might get divorced?" The answer is a resounding *no*. The "fight equals divorce" logic belongs to adults alone. The reality of parents in two different places never enters children's minds, no matter how much parents fight. Even teenagers who are more aware are still shocked that their parents are divorcing and moving into separate households. I have even heard people well into adulthood talk about their parents' divorce with deep shock at the idea of them not together. No wonder children are using any tactic to prevent the divorce. Unlike adults, they cannot function in the world alone and they are afraid of being abandoned.

As Ginny, age seven, put it, "If Daddy left, maybe Mommy will go and I'll be alone; who will take care of me?" In many ways, the essence of the divorce experience for children is exemplified in Ginny's fears. Unknowingly, she speaks volumes about how important it is to make sure our children feel secure, no matter what goes on.

Kevin's remarks, more of an announcement, to the group were greeted with great interest by his peers. While his comments may be shocking to some, variations on this theme happen every day in two-parent families. You know the drill: little Oscar corners Dad in the garage and asks if he can spend the night with a friend. He says no, so Oscar finds Mom in the kitchen and she says yes. In this family situation, Mom and Dad will eventually meet somewhere in the house, compare notes, and little Oscar is caught. But in a divorced family, the parents not only live in separate houses, but often don't communicate at all. Now we have a child in the middle with the power to create any story, true or not, to tell each parent. Add to this that both parents are courting Kevin to be with them. In this emotionally charged new situation, Mom and Dad are not rationally analyzing what Kevin is saying about each of them. Truly a perfect storm of miscommunication.

At this point, you might have a lapse of good sense and decide to share this insight about your own little power broker with your former husband. If you have little or no communication, or what you have is hostile, do not give in to this. No man wants to hear that he is being played by an eight-year-old and have this information delivered by his ex-wife! Do what you always do as mother-in-charge. Pay attention to what your child says and don't over-react. If your child is going back and forth between households, keep the conversation with your ex-husband factual, about schedules and arrangements. You can't stop the little messenger from trying to create confusion, but you can stop buying into it.

Kevin had developed a sophisticated way of dealing with his parents' divorce, but the experiences of Adam and the other children in the group were more common. Adam, age eight, joined the fray and added a new dimension to this already fascinating conversation with the following: "Mom always asks me about Dad after I've been to his house and then gets angry if she hears that he is going on a trip or has a new car. Then she's angry at me." This definitely resonated with the group, as many children clearly felt caught in the middle when questions answered truthfully that backfired on them. A number of children were confused that their mothers were so angry when they got back from Dad's – and got the message that they should not have fun there. If you are reading this, Mom, and see yourself, re-read Chapter Three until you can be a reasonably upbeat Mom. You sure can't change anyone's parenting but your own (my old song). You can control how you treat your child in regard to *not* putting her in the middle. Remember, your child is only caught in the middle if you both pull on him. When you stop pulling, it is no longer a tug of war.

When communication between divorced parents doesn't improve over the years, and children become teenagers, you often see one child become the go-between for parents. There is no family vote to elect this person, but it evolves gradually, and usually the most diplomatic child, the kind who listens to everyone, gets the role. As a mother, try very hard to prevent this from happening by not allowing your child to be put in this position. It creates a burden on teenagers and young adults who carry numerous expectations without much chance of success. Their role evolves from message carrier about school or visitation to the peace maker for a sibling and parent who don't communicate well. Encourage your children to each take responsibility for their own relationships and not put that responsibility on anyone else. Every family has that very kind mediator; do not use or abuse them.

It became painfully obvious in this session that many children, especially Amy, Kevin, Ginny, and Adam, had become the victims of their parents' unresolved marital issues, now manifested as "parenting issues," not "couple issues." The best way to prevent this is to go back to the basics, assume your mother-in charge role, and let your children be children: well-protected, secure, and loved.

To Become – An Insightful Woman

1. Never underestimate your child.
2. One person does not a tug-of-war make.
3. Never be blackmailed by a child.
4. Always make your child feel secure.

Chapter Five

Who Will Carve the Pumpkin? Holidays of all Kinds

Recently we attended the wedding of the son of dear, old friends. The last year had brought them a series of tragedies. The mother of the groom addressed the guests and said, "We can't get enough good times. We need to grab them and savor them; let the dancing begin." And begin it did, from her husband in a motorized wheelchair to the eighty-three-year-old great grandmother. It was a celebration of a marriage between two young people, but beyond that, a celebration of life and holding onto the good times.

Holidays are supposed to bring us these kind of warm feelings, but often in life the joy is lost in the planning, and stress replaces happiness as we try to bring everyone together for a Martha Stewart-like meal, without bloodshed. Add to this a recent divorce, and the additional planning and logistics, and pretty soon you want to forget the whole thing.

Well, if you are inclined to hide in your bed while the reindeer prance on the roof and turn off the porch light for trick-or-treaters, then remember my friend and about needing all the good times we can get. Even if you have turned into a Grinch, your children deserve these childhood memories, or else what stories will they have to tell when they get older?

No holiday in our house is complete without the retelling of some holiday adventure or misadventure that we experienced. There was the year we waited a bit too late to get a Christmas tree and traveled halfway across Florida to get one. Family tradition dictated that it must be real. There was the particularly memorable year that the Christmas tree fell down twice.

We suspected the family dog (more about him in Chapter Six), but he was never caught in the act. One Easter, I decided to serve an elegant Easter brunch with eggs Benedict, and I forgot the eggs. My kind family said the English muffin, sauce, and Canadian bacon was great. And of course, everyone has the carefully planned holiday dinner that involves one guest who drinks too much and turns dinner into a therapy session or a version of *Family Feud*. Look at it this way: who would want to be in a perfect family? They have no stories.

For whatever reason, I have always loved holidays. I made signs for my brother's birthdays and hung them around the house. I developed a fixation on Abraham Lincoln in middle school, and every February 12th, we had a log cake and Lincoln readings. As long as the log cake had lots of whipped cream, my girls were relatively tolerant of this event. But even a lover of holidays such as myself was apprehensive about my first holiday as a single mother, which turned out to be Halloween.

Now if you had to pick a first holiday alone as a threesome, Halloween is about the easiest. It is not drenched in expectations the way Thanksgiving and Christmas are. And, blessedly, food involvement is limited to purchasing candy for trick-or-treaters and sorting out the goodies your child brings home.

My greatest anxiety surrounded carving the pumpkin, something I had never done. Don't ask how I got into my thirties without carving a pumpkin, but I did. Each day, my daughter asked when I would carve the pumpkin and put a candle in it, like we always did. The only bright spot for me was that they seemed perfectly confident that I could handle this task. It is one of the great mysteries of life that we somehow deal with all the big issues in a divorce, like returning to work, while the small things like carving a pumpkin bring us to our knees.

As Halloween got closer, I realized that I was going through the motions and dreading the costumes, trick-or-treat, and mostly, that ever-present pumpkin. But I was convinced that none of this was visible to my children and a bright smile would be the answer. While we were picking out their holiday costume – a ritual second in importance only to selecting the birthday cake – my oldest daughter reached over and touched me and asked why I was sad. "Sad, I'm not sad," I said. "Yes you are," she said, "and I am, too."

As I looked into those deep brown eyes, I knew that she was looking for two things from me: honesty about my own feelings and permission to be sad. I realized that day that we had crossed into new territory as mother and daughter. A smile and cheerful words could not cover the real loss we had experienced; not just the loss of a father in the home, but a loss of childhood innocence that all is constant and secure and the most you have to worry about is keeping your sister out of your stuff.

That day we began to deal with the pain, loss, and separation experience that, as a mother, I had hoped would be years in the future for her. It became clear to me that I needed to be there for my children to help them sort it out, to listen, to give perspective, but most importantly, to reassure them that we could deal with this if we held on to each other and were honest. Children don't have problems with the honest part. We parents, however, do. I have learned through considerable trial and error that, no matter how difficult the truth is, it is always better than a lie.

This was certainly a lot of heavy stuff for the costume store, crushed between a Big Bird costume and a dancing bear, but I left that store with more insight about my new role, and I had my own child to thank.

I was energized to take charge and move us forward, and of course the first thing I encountered at home was . . . the uncarved pumpkin. With a burst of enthusiasm, I started to carve the pumpkin. I told the girls that the pumpkin's face would have a different look this year, but with a candle burning inside, he would do quite nicely for Halloween night. As I worked on his face, they sat attentively on the grass, relieved that I had finally gotten around to this task and eager to see the results. The finished product gave new meaning to the term "crooked smile." He actually looked like he'd had a facelift by a poorly trained plastic surgeon. My kids pronounced him a success, and with his candle, he was pleasantly off-center. But, most importantly, I did it. To this day, the picture of my small girls with the pumpkin is one of my all-time favorites and represents to me the beginning of healing and moving forward.

Halloween remains very special, and through the years, we started an annual Halloween party for our friends and their children, with chili and trick-or-treating. It became our annual celebration of good times. Look at your life and see what event could provide an opportunity to celebrate, and then plan your own event. Don't kill yourself trying to put on a big party. Start small. Make it easy on yourself (the chili was takeout, not homemade). And above all, have fun!

Halloween, Christmas, and Easter are all special for children, but nothing is quite as personal as your child's birthday. All the other holiday celebrations involve multiple activities, a tribe of relatives, religious observances, large family meals, frantic gift buying, and on and on. Your child's birthday, on the other hand, is his or her special day, and as such, gives you an opportunity to fuss over just them.

When my children were small, I started a ritual that still exists today, though obviously now in a different form, when distance and schedules allow. On their birthday, they were allowed to stay home from school and I took off work. The "birthday girl" set the agenda for the day: where we ate, what we did. Sometimes, the planning and discussing of possibilities was as much fun as the day itself. As you can imagine, in the early years, we went to McDonalds or the zoo, bought Barbie clothes, and ate ice cream. As they got older, we ate at local bistros and discovered Ann Taylor. But, no matter how the activities changed, one thing remained the same: sharing the day with a dear daughter on the anniversary of the day that she came into my life.

Another feature of the birthday is, of course, the planning of the birthday party. Unfortunately, today, many children's birthday parties have become a competition (between parents) of who has the most elaborate event: pony rides, clowns, etc. The kind of party I'm talking about is one that is fun and manageable for you and your child, not a community, little theatre production. First is the selection of the invitation. I have many happy memories of time spent debating the relative merits of a Winnie-the-Pooh party versus one with a Curious George theme. Then you select the napkins, plates, and accessories that carry out the theme.

In the center of the whole birthday process is the cake. In our family, we take the invitation to the bakery and have the cake made in its likeness. This particular tradition is rooted in my childhood. When I was growing up in New York City, I spent a lot of time with my maternal grandmother. As I look back on her now, she was ahead of her time in many ways. She went to college in an era when it was certainly not the norm for women, and she had a fun-loving, independent spirit. Whenever I was with her, we ate out. I honestly can't remember what her kitchen looked like. At the end of every outing, we stopped at Ebinger's Bakery in Brooklyn and I was allowed to select any dessert and have it in my own white box. She explained to me that she didn't bake because the baker had a family to support and we had a responsibility to support him. Sounded good to me, and I felt very special with my little white box with a string around it. As a result, our birthday cake tradition does not surround old family recipes, but bakeries.

The unconventional nature of this tradition did not hit me until an incident that occurred when my oldest was five years old. I picked her up from a friend's birthday party. As we were driving along, she was telling me how fun the party was, except for one thing, the cake. "The cake?" I asked. "What was wrong with it?" She replied, sadly, that her friend didn't have a *real* cake. Her mother had made it! Like the birthday cake, developing your own traditions is a matter of blending meaningful things from your past and creating new ones to add to it.

The month of December presents the greatest challenge in the holiday world. There should be a warning label on all women's magazines for the month of December that states: "This magazine is hazardous to the mental health of single mothers." They're not so hot for other working mothers, either. Nothing makes you feel more inadequate than pages of hand-sewn dresses, handmade ornaments, homemade wrapping paper (please), and recipes portrayed as easy holiday fun – with forty ingredients. Add to this guilt-inducing experience all the logistics of sharing children after a divorce, or worse yet, a father who does not appear at the appointed time, and you have a recipe for disaster and not a page from *The Walton's Christmas Book*.

At this point, you (remember mother-in-charge) have a decision to make. You can get completely overwhelmed by all this and turn into a grumpy Grinch who ignores the holiday. Or, you can rent the movie *Miracle on 34th Street,* pull yourself together, and make some fun plans for you and your children.

I happen to believe that Christmas is about children. It started with a baby in a manger and the wonder and joy of a small child will always be at the center of the Christmas experience. Only you and your children can decide what is most meaningful for you to do during this holiday season. With limited time and resources, plan some special things that you can look forward to and do together. A trip to the *Nutcracker* ballet was always a highlight of the season for us. Reading the story beforehand and planning what to wear made the anticipation half the fun. Also include something where your children make a decoration or do a picture for someone in a homeless shelter or nursing home. The concept of giving pleasure to others and those less fortunate than you is an important part of the whole holiday experience.

Ignore the things not on your holiday "to do" list. Your child will not go into therapy at forty if the Christmas cookie baking consists of cutting slices of frozen dough in a roll (a truly great invention) and drowning them in sprinkles. And believe me, in the rush of Christmas morning, no one will know or care if you made the wrapping paper or not.

Realistically, the first Christmas after a divorce is difficult and awkward. Whatever the circumstances, all of a sudden, the holidays are arrangements. A former routine when married, like two dinners in one day, thirty minutes apart, sounds like a piece of cake compared to the juggling of children between two or more households.

At this point, play that little tape in your head again – the one where you remind yourself that you cannot control what goes on anywhere but in your own home with your children. You cannot control how your ex-husband, his mother, your mother, your brother, his wife, etc., behave on the holiday, but you can control what *you* do. Things go a lot smoother when you don't have so much to control. Try and stay focused on the children and making this as easy on them as possible. This means stretching yourself. Dig down for your best self and try to make plans that cause the least conflict. This does not mean, however, sinking into a martyr role with guilt-inducing comments like, "Okay, spend the holidays with your dad. I'll just be here, all alone under the Christmas tree."

This is cruel to your children and doesn't do much for you as the mother-in-charge. Nothing will undo all your positive planning and fun with your children more than making them feel guilty because you're alone. Make sure you have plans for Christmas Eve or Christmas Day, whenever they are away. And be upbeat about those plans. I have been amazed to learn, as my children have grown up and we've talked about their childhood, how much they worried about me. Do not underestimate this. Holidays are fraught with expectations: those we create for ourselves, and those others try to create for us, past life expectations unfulfilled, and expectations and fears about an uncertain future. Divorce or no divorce, these feelings are part of the human experience, and holidays bring them into sharper focus. But, above all, holidays are celebrations. This is true whether they are the big ones such as Halloween and Christmas or the small one's we create out of everyday life that bring us joy.

These family celebrations are also not about being crafty or clever. If Martha Stewart herself was standing next to me helping me re-create an egg carton into a piece of art, mine would still look like an egg carton. It is about attitude and having a sense of fun and magic.

I will always remember one dreary weekend when my girls were young and it seemed like the rain would never end. We were all restless. One of the girls found some Chinese pajamas they had and I got the idea that we should have a Chinese tea party. We found another set of pajamas and a Kimono bathrobe that I had forgotten about. I braided their hair, and of course, make-up was required. An elegant table was set with ottoman and pillows. We drank tea and ate Chinese food, and finished the evening with fortune cookies. We forgot about the rain and being restless and had a celebration. Most things about that year have faded away, but not the memory of that day. As my wise friend said, "We can't get enough good times. We need to grab them and savor them." And create them, I'd like to add.

To Become – Joyful

1. Be honest with your children without sending the message, "Poor me."
2. Give your child special attention on his or her birthday, and be creative.
3. Keep the spirit and magic of the holidays alive – even if you don't feel it.
4. Create your own celebrations on ordinary days.

Chapter Six

I'm Dreaming of Bob Vila: Home Maintenance

As a school counselor in an elementary school, I started a group for children of divorced parents. Usually I worked with these children individually, so I wasn't sure what to expect when I brought eight children together to discuss their parents' divorce. Two things became immediately clear. First was that the divorce and the changes it brought to their lives had never been explained to them. Second was that they had a lot to say!

Their first comments, however, were not the ones I expected. I had anticipated hearing about feeling guilty that they caused the divorce, sad about Dad not being there, or the trouble it was to go between two houses. Instead, I heard that they were upset that, when their mothers were home, they didn't have time for them anymore because they were always cleaning or tidying up the house.

Nine-year-old Jenny added, "Whenever I want to tell Mom about school, she says she's too busy because she has to work around the house, since it's just her to take care of things now." So Jenny decided to "help" her mom. She got on a chair and started to wash the dishes. Then her mother, whom she thought would be pleased, came running around the corner, yelling at her to get down before she fell. Jenny was almost in tears, relating to the other children that her mother said she had a lot on her mind and Jenny needed to be extra good and not make mommy worry. Jenny didn't try to help again and her mother continued to do her chores around the house: a lost opportunity for mother and daughter to connect.

Obviously, there are always household chores to be done, married or divorced. But some women react to stress by turning into compulsive cleaners, like Heloise on steroids. The children in my group all felt shut out by their mother's obsession with an orderly house and frustrated by their inability to really help their mother. The motivation behind the Heloise Syndrome is as simple as it is sad. If I cannot have the orderly, tidy life that I had, thought I had, or wanted, then I will create the most orderly, tidy house that I can. Housework is a good place to hide. It is certainly easier to scrub a kitchen floor than to explain things you don't understand yourself to a child. And, if you were brought up in the tradition of a spotless home as a standard of a good wife and mother, then it is twice as hard for you to alter your housekeeping standards, spend time with your children, and ignore the rest.

Since self-reflection is a large component of becoming a single mother, this would be a good time to look at how you were raised in regard to "keeping house," and what messages about that role you have carried into you adult life. Understanding yourself in this regard is a first step toward creating a balance between obsessive house-keeper and being a complete slob. Fortunately for me, my upbringing did not create any great expectations in regard to home maintenance. My three brothers and I grew up in New York, in an apartment, and my mother could not send four small children outside to play while she did housework. She made the choice to take us to the park to play, safe in the knowledge that any household chores would still be there when she returned. In addition, everything in our apartment that broke, popped a leak, or made a strange sound was fixed by Tom, the building manager. He seemed to appear almost instantly with tools in hand, to fix whatever the crisis of the day was. Our father was great fun, spent endless hours with us in games and imaginative play, but he was genetically unable to do even simple repair tasks. Dad would be in the living room reading poetry while Mom and Tom manned the front lines of domestic maintenance. I'm sure my mother had help from time to time with housework, but my memory about such activities is dim. It was always true in our house that time spent doing things together always trumped housework. When company was coming, we all were expected to pitch in and help, and things got done. If it sounds like it was a bit chaotic, it was, especially when "the group clean" was in progress. But somehow it all worked out.

This all worked for us for a long time, until we moved to Minnesota from New York City when I was in high school. It was our first family venture of living in a house, and I remember my parents standing in the front yard discussing who would take care of all this. It was a small yard, but to the couple who had never had a yard, it looked like Central Park. Since my dad doing the work was not an option, they somehow found Mr. Higgins, who replaced Tom, the building manager, and life resumed. Until one day not long after starting their new school, my brothers returned home in tears. It turned out that they were being teased because we had Mr. Higgins to work around our house. My brother Jim asked who these teasers had fix things in their house and they said their dads did it! My brother would have more easily believed that little green men lived in the backyard than believe that dads could fix anything. So began our eye-opening life in the Midwest, where it seemed everyone could clean, polish, scrub, sand, and varnish anything with ease, and such activities were on the level of an art form. It goes without saying that none of this rubbed off on our family. Years later, as a recently divorced young mother, I stood in the front yard of my house in Florida and asked the same question my parents had asked so long ago: "Who is going to take care of all this?" They had each other to find an answer. I was talking to myself.

My first household challenge was a yard that had gotten unruly when the lawn mower and its human operator left. Adopting what would become a lifelong coping strategy for house related things I could not handle immediately; I took a deep breath and ignored it – placing it on the bottom of the list of things to cope with. One day, a neighbor came by and said his sons were looking to gain yard work experience and they'd like to practice on my lawn, well on its way to becoming a jungle. I knew this was not true, but I was deeply grateful for the concern and help. The yard was mowed that day, and this young man and other young men in the neighborhood became my lawn crew. For a modest amount, they kept the jungle at bay.

Once, the small bath by our utility room was broken and I did not have the extra time or money for a plumber. The girls and I decorated a sign that said "Out of Order," and it stayed that way until I could fix it. Ignoring household things you can't immediately fix keeps you from stewing over things that are less important than your children's welfare and your time with them.

Abandon the Martha Stewart version of the perfect home and whatever mother-messages you have on this topic and begin to set your own reasonable, attainable standards for home upkeep. As you develop these new standards, engage your children as partners in keeping up your joint home. If the mother of my student Jenny had taken this approach, she and her daughter could have worked together on the dishes and their relationship at the same time. The secret to having children help you is two-fold: to select tasks they can do with minimal assistance, and letting them do it in whatever way they can, while not *criticizing*. In my children's divorce group, there was a common theme about helping mom that was best expressed by seven-year-old Tim. "Everything that I do to help Mommy is always wrong."

Of course, a seven-year-old setting the table will not complete it in the perfectly orderly way you do; but that's really not the point, is it? Children need to feel they can contribute and experience success and not failure. So the place mats are crooked and don't match, there are all spoons and no forks, and all the glasses are old sippie cups. Who cares? No one does. The dinner table police will not be knocking on your door, and best of all, your child will glow with pride. Little Timmy would have been happy to have just one successful moment, when Mom praised him for his good help. Look at it this way: eating with all spoons is possible, and a sippie cup without the lid is quite manageable. It's a small price to pay for your child's self-esteem.

Shortly after my husband moved out, my girls wanted to share a room. Fixing up their joint room and making the extra room into a playroom was a therapeutic project in itself. They might not be able to control the physical changes within the house, as Dad's absent belongings left gaps in various rooms, but they could control what happened in these two rooms. We had a good time moving furniture, clothes, etc. But the most fun surrounded the purchase of a green frog toy box for the new playroom. The three of us found it in a toy store together and it was one of those things that called to you to take it home. It had a big lid and two large frog eyes, and it served not only as a toy box, but as a hiding place and a place to just sit amidst all the stuffed animals. The whole bedroom-playroom project kept us busy and was a wonderful way to transition out life. In a time-stressed single parent household, household tasks can be accomplished with your children as helpers.

Another bit of wisdom about the children's view of things at the time of divorce came when six-year-old Amanda burst out one day, "I want my bear and blanket every night, but Mommy says now that we're alone, I need to put them away and be a big girl." Other six-year-olds less forthright about their need for these items just nodded in agreement. Sometimes we become so focused on our own need for comfort (be it food, drink [bad idea], or a day in bed) that we forget that children have the same needs at a different level. Amanda can't compulsively clean a floor or create a rigid schedule to give her life structure and security, but her need is the same and can be met with her same blanket and bear and her little possessions in the same place. The worst message in Amanda's mother's comment is that now that Dad and I are no longer together, you can't be a child anymore and need to grow up. Sadly, just the fact of the situation will cause her to grow up to some extent, but she is still the child and *you* are the parent. (Refer to Chapter One) You are the mother-in-charge, not part of a parent-child parenting team! Parenting, and especially single parenting, is not a democracy.

If you ever need inspiration to keep the compulsive tidy-fairy at bay, just remember that Jenny, Tim, Amanda, and your own children, at age forty, will not remember if the baseboards were cleaned weekly, but they will remember that day you took time to have a spur of the moment picnic at the park, chased shadows down the street, or sat on the beach holding them and singing songs while the sun went down.

To Become – Realistically Tidy

1. Talk to your children about the divorce and let them ask questions; give them real answers.
2. Cancel your subscription to *Martha Stewart Living* and set realistic housekeeping expectations for your home.
3. Involve your children in maintaining your mutual home.
4. In adulthood, your children will remember their time with you, not a well scrubbed house.

Chapter Seven

The Dearly Departed Thumper the Rabbit: Pets, Alive and Otherwise

Next to a white picket fence, there is no image that signals "happy family resides here" more than the sight of children romping in the yard with Fido, the family dog. In these bucolic scenes, Fido is clean and well-groomed, as are the children, as they roll around in the grass in a playful game of Frisbee. In the logic of newly divorced single-motherhood, the presence of Fido would be comforting, even if Dad is gone. Go figure; it's not like their roles were the same.

In fact, when the subject of pets came up with the children's group, a couple of children became agitated because a favorite pet was given away after the divorce. Tommy, age eight, addressed it best. "Milo, our dog, was my best friend and he slept with me. Late at night when I woke up because Mom and Dad were fighting, I buried my face in Milo's fur so I couldn't hear." As Tommy talked more, it emerged that Tommy's mother gave Milo to a family friend because she said she was too busy to fuss with a dog and he was Dad's dog, anyway.

While I've talked about simplifying your life, I never meant to eliminate a family member, and that's what Milo was: a family member. Tommy's mother, unintentionally I'm sure, was punishing Tommy for his parent's divorce and depriving him of a great source of comfort at a time he needed it most. Perhaps anger at her ex-husband played a role in this decision as she referred to Milo as "Dad's dog." This is exactly why you must get your feelings in perspective about your ex-husband because the anger can erupt when you least expect it and hurt the child you love, in this case, Tommy.

If there has never been a Fido in the house, then to rush out and purchase a dog or any other pet requires serious thought and deliberation, not an emotional reaction to the notion that some pet will give the illusion of normal family life. Somehow, I bought into the notion that I owed my children a pet. This thought never occurred to me as a married woman. But as a single mother, I felt the animal experience was a crucial part of their childhood experiences. Guilt popped up its ugly head again, this time in the form of a pet.

Thus began our animal phase, during which, over the next couple of years, we managed to go through, and I don't use this term lightly, a variety of pets, including, but not limited to:

Dogs: Tabatha; Casey

Cats: Priscilla; Mr. Miskafoles (found on the front steps after we had seen the play *Cats*)

Rabbit: Thumper

Parakeet: Radar

Hamsters/Gerbils: Happy I, II, III, & IV; Frisky

Fish: too numerous to name

Guinea Pig

Hermit Crabs

Animal-Like Experiences: Ant Farm; Butterfly Garden (the best of all!)

If the purpose of this pet parade was to distract us from other things, then it certainly succeeded.

My pet experiences as a child were very limited, and for the most part, unsuccessful. I grew up with three younger brothers and no dogs or cats to entertain us or be entertained by us. Our New York apartment building did allow pets, but apparently our parents felt that the four of us provided all the entertainment they wanted or could handle. The first pet I ever wanted was a painted turtle at the circus. My father had taken the four of us by himself on the subway to Madison Square Garden for some parent-child bonding under the Big Top. On entering the Garden, I immediately saw the turtles and had to have one. Of course, my brother chimed in for one, as well. We spent the entire circus playing with our turtles, trying to get them to race and fight with each other, ignoring the main event in the center ring. The poor turtles only lasted a few days, probably raced or loved to death. By the way, my father never again ventured out with us alone; we bonded at home.

One Easter, a patient of my father's gave us live chicks. We had a small patio and we put them out there, completely fascinated by them. Then, for reasons that are unclear, we decided to give them a bath. Unsupervised just long enough to dip them in a tub of water, we quickly discovered that chicks did not need or want a bath, and did not survive our attention.

It suffices to say that my pet track record was less than stellar, and yet, as a new single mother, ignoring experience and going with hope, I got our first pet. The new family member was a rabbit named Thumper. It is unclear how we settled upon a rabbit, but my youngest daughter, Laura, liked the idea best and with little factual information to object, her sister and I agreed. At first, his hopping around the house was cute. His inability to be housetrained never was, and he continued to grow and grow. As a little bunny, he fit in my four-year-old's dress pocket and this entertained her to no end. Making sure Thumper had food and water was a job in itself. My daughters were too young to assume this responsibility, so guess who became the single parent to two girls and a rabbit? You guessed right. As our family pet grew, we got a cage for him to be in the backyard where he could play safely (or so we thought), undisturbed by neighborhood children or predatory pets. Thumper was happily playing in his cage one late fall day, when, as an unseasonable thunderstorm came up, Thumper's cage was struck by lightning. I'll spare you the ugly details of what it was like when we returned home and the girls ran to the backyard, carrots in hand to see Thumper, because we don't want to imagine that scene! What started out as lesson in caring for a pet, upon the demise of Thumper, became a lesson in sudden death.

Our next pet experience was thrust upon us not long after the Thumper episode. Radar the parakeet was a gift from the girls' father. He never wanted pets when we were together, so maybe I wasn't the only one with this strange logic that made pets a dad stand-in. Laura was delighted to have Radar living in her room, but it became quickly apparent that she had developed an allergy, and the only new element in her life was Radar. A visit to the ever-attentive pediatrician, J.K., confirmed that her wheezing was due to Radar. So I set about finding him a new home and explaining to her father that Radar was re-locating for medical reasons. One day, in the midst of this venture, I looked at my "to do list" and saw that number 2 was "find Radar a good home" and laughed. I was beginning to roll with the unexpected and getting to know (albeit briefly) more animals then I was ever exposed to as a child.

The whole process of acquiring pets, naming them, and giving them the best home that we could became a three-way venture for us. Don't get too excited here; while the girls did learn some pet responsibility, I was the one responsible for overseeing the whole process.

In this realm, we learned a few things, often the hard way. If you take these things to heart they may save you a lot of trouble:

1. Cats do not like to walk on a leash. Although it was fun to watch the girls try.
2. Fish do not remain healthy (or alive) if fed ten times a day.

3. Hermit Crabs – well they are just grumpy and anti-social.
4. Hamsters can easily be mistaken for a mouse when running quickly around the house. (One time, a babysitter drove what she thought was a mouse outside, only to discover upon my return that Happy II had escaped from his cage. Apparently, his cage door was left ever so slightly ajar by a small visitor checking on him.)
5. Ant farms are fascinating to watch, until outdoor ants are added to the farm. After a neighbor child put a few handfuls of dirt into the farm, the battle between the ant farm ants and the "outsiders" looked like a battle scene from the History Channel. The outsiders won – there were no survivors.
6. Puppies (Tabatha and Casey) require the same consistent love and discipline as children. The truth is that, given my lack of animal experience and the responsibilities that I already had, I did not have the time, energy, or skill to raise well-adjusted, well-behaved dogs. I never did quite adjust to the fact that at the pediatrician office I had children on the well-behaved side of things and at the veterinarian it was a different story. It was necessary for me to remind myself that this dog situation was not a failure, but a realistic assessment of my limitations.

At the end of the day, Barbara and Laura did become acquainted with all kinds of pets, and they did learn to care for them after a fashion. But I take comfort in the fact that all our pets were loved, some loved to death, but all loved. We never did have the Fido of my dreams, rolling around the front yard and playing Frisbee with the children. Tabatha and Casey would always run away if we let them out in the front yard alone. Barbara, Laura, and I can laugh at the memory of adventures with Thumper or Priscilla. Our animal care was not perfect (just ask the overfed fish) but we did it together.

To Become – A Pet Mother

1. Neither the dog nor the cat will fill the void of a departed father.
2. Be prepared to be mother-in-charge of pets and children.
3. Select a pet you can manage – not ponies or snakes.
4. Remember, no hermit crabs – only pets that can love you back.

Chapter Eight

Purple Eye Shadow and Green Hair: Thirteen is Thirteen, Divorce or No Divorce

In my children's divorce group, one of the older children (in this case, older being fourth grade), Jason had a reputation for telling all his teachers, when confronted with misbehavior or poor class work, that he couldn't help it, he was a child of divorce. At this tender age, Jason had already discovered that he could offload his behavior to divorce, absolving himself of any responsibility for his actions. Believe me, he did not come up with this concept and that wording on his own. Some adult in his family had been singing the same song. Shortly after this, his grandmother, who assumed a great deal of his care, came in for a parent conference. The very first thing she told me, before I could say a word, was that Jason should have special consideration in his school behavior because he was a child of divorce. His grandmother had handed him a great line. In the world of fourth grade boys, any excuse will do. Children at this age are too young to be moved to accomplish schoolwork by discussions of what they'll do when they grow up, how they'll support themselves, or what skills they will need. One of my brothers spent his entire fourth grade year drawing battleships with dead bodies hanging off them. If my parents had been divorced, everyone would have claimed his behavior was the result of his broken home. He would have made the case that the trauma of separated parents and two households drove him to the dead battleship routine. The facts are far less interesting. He was creative, bright, bored, and liked his battleships with bodies strewn about. He was also a fourth grade boy, not given to great introspection about his life.

All children go through certain stages of development, whether you are divorced or not. Toddlers walk between eleven and eighteen months, two-year-olds say "no" a lot, and teenagers . . . well, use your imagination. In addition to the basic stages of development, all children are born with their own unique personalities. One of my divorce class children, Brian, age eight, was solemn, quiet, studious, and shy. It would be easy to go "Ah ha, divorce has taken its toll." In fact, Brian's mother said he was like that from birth, a solemn boy who smiled little but seemed content. His parents divorced when he was seven, and he was solemn and shy, just as he had always been. Brian's parents would have had cause for real concern if Brian, normally placid, had suddenly started fighting with other children and acting out against his parents. Then his parents would have reason to worry. The family divorce might be the cause, but so might other things, such as bullying at school or learning problems, to name just two. It is easy for divorced parents to assume that their situation is the cause of any problems (guilt pops up so easily), but you owe it to your child and to yourself to explore all possibilities.

Since I spent many sleepless nights as a single mother pondering these questions, I came up with three questions that I think can at least get your nighttime anxiety organized in some productive way.

1. What is your child's basic personality?
   Was your child a peaceful baby – content in the crib – or was your child very active and crying for attention from the start?
2. What is normal development and behavior for your child's age?
   If you are expecting a twelve-month-old to be toilet trained, then you are expecting a behavior for which they're not developmentally ready.

3. Are there any sudden changes in your child's behavior that concern you?
   If your normally non-stop talking and story-telling child is suddenly quiet and withdrawn, then something must have happened and you should seek out the cause.

In my single parenting classes, we spent a lot of time focusing on these questions. A class member, Jean, who was twenty-six and the mother of three young girls, shared that pondering these questions at least got her panic organized and got her to think about her children and not just stress over them.

Since there are three questions to ponder, I've developed three approaches that should help you find your own answers to these questions and help you in your quest to be a competent mother-in-charge.

I. Trust your instincts about your child.

I always joke with my family that I might not notice if the grass was cut for a few weeks, but I always notice the emotional climate in the family, a subtle change in someone's mood or behavior. If you feel in your inner self that something is not right with your child, you are usually correct. Pay attention to your children, observe their normal habits and fears, and keep track of your child's behavior while trying to anticipate their next move. Mothers do have innate instincts about their children, but they aren't fully developed the day your child is born. They unfold over time by carefully observing, listening to, and loving your children.

I remember when I was pregnant with my oldest daughter, I had a friend, Ginny, who had a one-month-old boy. She claimed she could tell by Justin's cry whether he was in pain, hungry, or just bored. I could not hear any difference in his cries and went home discouraged about my ability to be a good mother. My poor baby was going to have to move to Ginny's house to get decent care. A year later, when my own precious Barbara had arrived and settled in, or should I say taken over, much to my surprise and relief, I could hear the difference in her cries.

I never think about this whole issue of instinct without being reminded of my own sister-in-law who lives in California. When her son was ten, he began complaining about a pain in his chest; always a quiet child, Jimmy had never been a complainer. His mother took him to the doctor a couple of times and each time she was told that it was probably a strained muscle from playing baseball and that it was nothing to be concerned about. My sister-in-law, on the other hand, knew her child well. She had those instincts, but most important in this case, she trusted them and despite the doctor's reassurance, she was convinced that all was not well. One day, Jimmy said the pain had started again, and this time she called the doctor's office and demanded that he not only be seen, but that some tests be done to check out his condition. My usually gentle and soft-spoken sister-in-law must have terrified the doctor with her outburst, but she got his attention. While the doctor made it clear that he was quite sure nothing was wrong, he agreed to see her at once. He suggested that she put a hot compress on her son's chest to ease the pain on their way to the office. By the time they arrived at the doctor's office, to the shock and horror of everyone, the heat had drawn out a tumor in his chest. He had a very rare form of cancer. After years of treatment and pain, he emerged cancer-free, and just recently, he and his wife adopted a little boy. Thanks to my sister-in-law's instincts about her child, and her actions, she saved her son's life. Hopefully your actions as a mother will not need to be that dramatic, but they are important to the physical and mental well-being of your child.

II. Take advice from family, friends, and all other well-meaning people with a grain of salt (sometimes a whole shaker).

One of the unexpected things that happened when I became a single mother was that all sorts of people, from close family members to mere acquaintances, felt compelled to give me unsolicited advice about raising my children. Something about me being without a husband made everyone feel comfortable to barge in with their opinions. I mentioned this Dr. Phil-like phenomenon in my single parenting class and everyone began talking at once and laughing. I had clearly hit a nerve, one of those common experiences that people don't always share. (Another one is the fact that, in my newly single state, only married men asked me out, but more about that later.) We were agreed that while we were laughing now, we did not consider it funny at the time. When you're at your point of lowest self-esteem and worried about how you will manage with your children anyway, the last – very last – thing you need is some frightening situation presented to you under the guise of "helpful concern."

The following are a couple of examples chosen from a very large (too large, in my opinion) pool of available stories that came from our class that night.

Well-meaning friend number 1 (next door neighbor)

"Your Tammy doesn't walk yet? Well when my cousin's son didn't walk by fifteen months, it was because he had a serious nerve disease. Maybe you should look into that." Just when you think you've managed to conjure up every awful thing imaginable – rainy, long nights set the right mood for this – someone comes along and presents you with a new worry. Nerve disease as a reason for not walking at fifteen months? I just thought he had nowhere to go yet! The fact is that the normal range for walking is quite large, anywhere from ten to twenty months. If you carry your child around a lot, or if older siblings get everything for them, there's not much motivation to walk. Let's avoid well meaning friend number 1 in the future.

II. Well-meaning friend number 2 (car pool mother who never smiles)

"Your little Angie doesn't talk yet and she's two? She must be retarded." Well, there is a big leap from not talking at two and being developmentally delayed. One of my closest friends had a daughter who never spoke a word except Mommy and Daddy until she was two years and two months. At two years and two months and two weeks, she opened her mouth and began speaking in sentences; no single words here. She hasn't stopped talking yet!

III. Well-meaning friend number 3 (actually the grandmother)

"I told my friend Mildred that my grandson, Johnny, was a middle schooler and had big mood swings. One day he acted like a baby. The next day he thought that he was grown-up. Mildred says he is probably depressed and needs drugs." Children between ten and thirteen are called "middle schoolers" for a reason. They are literally in the middle between childhood and adolescence. They really do have mood swings. One day, the childhood side is in control and they want to curl up with an old, stuffed animal. The next day, adolescence is in control and they want their mother to drop them off three blocks from school so no one will see them with Mom. Little Johnny is not necessarily depressed or in need of drugs. His behavior is appropriate for his age, even if it drives you crazy.

IV. Well-meaning friend number 4 (your former mother-in-law)

"My neighbors' sixteen-year-old son, Todd, is not handling his parents' divorce very well. He wants to spend most of his time with his friends and not at home." Divorce or no divorce, sixteen-year-old boys generally prefer to be with their own peer group and not with their parents. At sixteen, your child is trying to assert some independence and make a life not solely made up of family members. Relax, Mom! Let him spread his wings a bit.

Our class came to the conclusion that night that some people just love to tell the most awful, gruesome tales and one's mental health requires avoiding these people as much as possible. Or, if that's not possible, train yourself to ignore them!

3. Find a good pediatrician and never, never let him or her go.

Friends, even husbands, may come and go, but your real partner in raising your children is their pediatrician. After my daughters were grown and I would see their pediatrician, Dr. J.K. David, at social gatherings, I would always tell people that "we" raised my girls. It is completely true, for without his calm, kind, and knowledgeable support, my single parent years would have been far more difficult.

The most important word in the last sentence is calm. No one needs a hysterical pediatrician making you more nervous, if that's possible. When Dr. David was recommended to us, my friend said, "He is so calm that if you told him your child was run over by a truck, he'd tell you to move the truck and meet him at the emergency room." There is nothing scarier as a single mother than having your child sick with no other adult to share the stress. It doesn't help if it's late, dark, and yes, raining.

What always amazed me about J.K. (everyone's name for Dr. David) was how no question ever seemed too stupid. If he was laughing, you sure couldn't tell. For example, one of our hamsters bit my older daughter while she and her sister were playing with him. It was not a severe bite, but enough to break the skin. The next morning, Frisky was dead in his cage. Immediately, I assumed that Frisky died of a terrible disease which he passed on to my daughter with the bite. My first course of action was to call our faithful pediatrician, J.K. He called me back quickly and said he doubted that our dear pet had any rare or terrible disease, but if it made me feel better, I could take him to the health department to be tested.

It just so happened that this was the same day I had to bring a "treat" for the teacher's lounge at school, a primitive custom that guarantees that no one can ever lose weight. Halfway to the health department, I looked down at the front seat and started laughing out loud at the nice tray of cookies (bakery purchased, of course) sitting next to a box with a dead hamster. It actually summed up my life at that point; one minute I'm a capable teacher/mother, and the next minute a CSI detective looking for a the cause of a hamster's death. What else is there to do but laugh!

Over the years, J.K. was always there to reassure me when my fear was greater than the medical crises at hand, like the hamster incident. He was also there to get me through a scary viral illness in my older daughter and to diagnose a rare eye disease in my twelve-year-old child. Long after my youngest grew up and moved overseas, J.K. sent me articles about her eye disease and new treatments being developed. He had great respect for his young patients and, by some miracle, for crazed mothers like me. I told him once shortly before he died that every time I came to him in those single mother years, I wasn't my real self. My real self was rational and sensible. He smiled and patted my hand and said, "Your behavior fit the situation; you were fine – just fine." That was way too generous, but I loved hearing it anyway.

Keep looking until you find a J.K. – someone you can talk to and feel comfortable with – and above all, trust with your precious, sick children. Don't stay with any doctor who makes you feel stupid, dismisses your questions, or doesn't respect you and you children. How do you find such a pediatrician? Talk to friends with children, pay attention to their experiences, and then go interview potential physicians. When you are interviewing a potential pediatrician, don't be intimidated. Remember, you know when someone is talking down to you and dismissing your observations and questions. Don't accept that. Move on. Talk to more pediatricians. Your J.K. is out there.

One of the pitfalls of single motherhood is that our own feelings (loss, guilt, etc.) tend to make us attribute all childhood issues to the divorce, preventing us from seeing other powerful forces in our child's life. In the single parenting class, the night we had this funny and sad conversation, a number of other issues arose from the group. One man, John, shared that his own parents' divorce as a child did not tear him apart the way his unathletic manner, gangly look, and poor social skills defined his high school years. To this day, John still cringes at the memory of having no one accept his invitation to the prom. I'm amazed at how often I hear people, long past those years, still recounting high school trauma.

So take heart, Mom, there are lots of things out there to traumatize your children besides your marital situation. As a mother, pay attention to the culture your child is living in at school and in the neighborhood. Learn about your child's friends; open your eyes. John claimed that his mother never knew about his tortured high school years. She just passed it off as the divorce. Don't fall into this trap. You owe it to your child to do better.

When all else fails and you hit a brick wall, call your J.K.

To Become – An Observant Mother

1. Every child has his or her own unique personality, so learn it and accept it.
2. Trust and act on your instincts about your child.
3. Smile but don't take to heart horror stories.
4. Find a good pediatrician and never, never let him or her go.

Chapter Nine

Scrambled Eggs for Dinner: Culinary Tips Not Found in Gourmet Magazine

There are some tasks than can be ignored temporarily (like the small broken bathroom that I put a "Out of Order" sign on) or done intermittingly (like laundry), but there is one task that must be faced not only every day, but worse yet, three times a day. Well-known author Pat Conroy talks about his own rather abrupt introduction to cooking in his book, *The Pat Conroy Cookbook*:

> I had come to cooking by accident and it was one of the strangest events in my life when I found myself before a stove with three daughters wandering around me fully expecting that I would feed them before I put them to bed.

Therein lies the problem. There are expectations, not unreasonable, on the part of children that regular meals will occur. I can remember a day when I was weary from work and suggested that we have scrambled eggs for dinner. You would have thought I had suggested that we not get a Christmas tree or that we stomp on the Halloween pumpkin. There was a loud chorus of two small people shouting, "We can't eat scrambled eggs for dinner. That's for breakfast." I figured this was not a good time (as they were hungry) or the right audience (they were five and eight) to discuss the subtle difference between maintaining tradition and being creative about food groups.

Shortly after that rather strong reaction from my children about appropriate food, I brought up the whole topic of food and family dinners to my fourth grade group of children of divorce. Now here was a topic everyone wanted to talk about! First of all, every child could tell you what food was in the house: if they were out of milk, crackers were low, or worst of all, if there was little food there at all. One dark-haired girl, Mona, explained it best when she said, "I feel so good when the refrigerator is full." The rest of the group nodded in agreement. It was revealing that they were not looking for children's favorites like cookies or candy, but they just wanted the refrigerator full.

The young ones, without knowing it, had touched upon a deep, universal truth: food is not just about meat and potatoes laden with butter and salt, but laden with feelings and memories of warmth, home, caring, love, and security, or a longing for these things never experienced. It became obvious as Mona and her fourth grade friends discussed this further that the full cupboard and refrigerator made them feel secure. It is a good time to remember that no matter how stressful you find your new single status, at least you can get to the store, buy a candy bar, and get a Starbucks. Children faced with an empty refrigerator can't go to the store and buy food or prepare it. This is a stark reminder that your child's sense of security is solely dependent on the physical and emotional security that we as mothers provide. It is also important to remember that children are very literal (hence scrambled eggs as a breakfast food). They take what we say at face value. For example, if you are constantly saying, "I don't have any money," then children don't think that you maybe haven't been to the bank or that you forgot your debit card, but that you literally have no money. This information, combined with the lack of groceries in the house, and they assume that the lack of money caused the empty cupboard. Suddenly, children feel less secure and helpless to do anything to feed themselves, or you. Remember, this is a child's thought process, and to understand them, we must get in tune with it.

If it is true that you don't have any money and are in a crisis, it becomes imperative that you do not unduly worry your children. It is fine to share with them that money is tight right now and that some things we enjoy doing or having may have to wait awhile, but your children should not become the sounding board for your anxiety over a looming electric bill or car payment. Obviously the age of the child dictates how much detail you share, but no matter how old your children are, *you* are the responsible parent and *they* are the cared-for child.

Another element of the children-food conversation concerns the mood at mealtime. A very outgoing child, John, declared that dinnertime used to be fun at his house, a time when his parents laughed. Now, he said, his mother looks sad and no one sits in Dad's chair. When I met John's mother a few weeks later, she told me that John had gotten hard to manage lately and that he refused to eat his dinner. No surprise there, for it sounds like family dinner has turned into a grim affair with sad Mom and Dad's empty chair. I think I would have lost my appetite, as well. One of the children in the group suggested that John put some stuffed animals in Dad's chair. There is something wonderful about coping strategies that come from the nine-year-old set.

In an effort to prove themselves the mother-in-charge, many single mothers seem to think they have to be good at everything, even things they were not interested in or good at before. This, in case you've ever wondered, is what "over compensation" means. It has always been true for me that, given the choice between cooking or reading a book, I will always pick reading a book. Reading relaxes me. Cooking is an effort. A close friend of mine is just the opposite. Her idea of relaxing is a long, complicated recipe that keeps her occupied in the kitchen for hours. The mere thought of that makes me tired. It is fun to make holiday dinners and plan the ever-important birthday party, but the regular, daily meal preparation that raising children requires is just plain work. This, however, does not keep me from collecting numerous cookbooks and constantly clipping recipes out of magazines. Occasionally, I surprise even myself (not to mention my family) with some great meals from one of these recipes.

Day-to-day meal preparation is not about perfect dinners and table settings, but about all of you being together and sharing a meal, whatever it might be. If you are a fan of the television show *Desperate Housewives*, then you know that the perfectly prepared and presented meals by desperate housewife Bree Vandercamp do nothing to compensate for the chilly and stiff atmosphere at the dinner table with her family. It is important that you all sit down together and eat, for in those moments, you connect with your child and share your day. Even if it's fast food, bring it home, sit at the table, and talk.

My own early years impressed upon me the importance of eating together, not necessarily the importance of what we eat. My father was a child psychiatrist, and for a number of years, he was the medical director for a state hospital in New York. We lived in an apartment (no kitchen) on the grounds and ate all three meals in the dining room with other doctors, nurses, and staff who resided there, as well. As a child, this arrangement seemed normal and fun. It wasn't until I was a mother myself that I realized how challenging this must have been to my mother. Eating in our pajamas was not an option, and we did need to behave. The good news was that we all ate together every night. Despite his responsibilities, our father ate with us every night. At first there were two of us children (ages three and one). Eventually, there were four. Our favorite culinary treat was to collect all the lemon wedges for iced tea (unsweet tea my southern-friends) and pour sugar over them and suck them. We also did creative things with linen napkins that even Martha Stewart hadn't thought about. Those were fun times together. I cannot recall any food except the lemon escapades, but it was the highlight of every day.

Even the most cooking-challenged mother can make use of two critical bits of culinary information gleaned from my children groups, my own children, and the child I used to be. First, keep the refrigerator and cupboards full with cans of vegetables, boxes of cereal, juice, etc. Once I realized this was such a big deal with children (my own included), I shopped with an eye toward filling up the shelves and refrigerator. When I think of all the time we spend as mothers trying to make children feel secure, it is good to know that a small part of this can be accomplished at the grocery store. Who knew?

The second bit of childhood wisdom is that the mood surrounding a meal is more important than the food itself. John's mother, who was always depressed at dinner, was putting her own self-pity before the needs of her child. There is magic and a sense of fun about children that shouldn't be lost in the day-to-day of even a stressful life. The child who suggested that John put stuffed animals in his dad's chair had the magic. I like to think some of it rubbed off on John's mom.

Since I promised you a culinary tip in this chapter, here it is. Remember the bakery birthday cake in Chapter Four? Well, it tastes best the second day, after a night in the refrigerator, accompanied by a glass of cold milk. Trust me on this one. Cake for breakfast, anyone? Just keep in mind that cake for breakfast is a rare, once-a-year treat for your child's birthday. The rest of the year, mother-in-charge must purchase healthy foods, prepared as simply as possible, and presented with love. I guess that's two culinary tips.

To Become – A Good Kitchen Witch

1. Food equals security, so keep the cabinets and refrigerator full.
2. Make it a top priority to eat together every night and share the day.
3. Prepare simple and healthful meals – this is not a Pillsbury Bake-Off competition.
4. When time permits, cook with your children, as the food is less important than the shared activity.

Chapter Ten

Tick Tock – It's Six O'clock: Childcare for all Ages

In the tale of Cinderella, the magic hour is midnight, when Cinderella will turn from a beautiful girl into a scullery maid and, worst of all, lose her glass slipper. For single working mothers, the magic hour is six p.m. when their childcare provider is ready to close and late charges are added to her fee (some $5 per minute). In addition to the money, a late mother is guilt personified as her little one sits alone with the last childcare worker. This scene makes Cinderella losing her glass slipper look easy. Across this county every afternoon between five and six p.m., there is a large group of working parents ready to begin "the six o'clock race." This group can be identified by other people because they are flying, not walking, out of office buildings, driving with hands clutching the steering wheel, staring straight ahead, foot heavy on the gas. They are on a mission – make it to destination childcare by six p.m. The sudden appearance of a train or a long line of traffic can cause a massive anxiety attack manifested by sweaty palms and clenched teeth. The only thing that separates all working parents from single mothers is that single mothers have no spouse to call to see if they can make it to Puddle Ducks Day Care on time. There are no water stops for those in the six o'clock race, and definitely no t-shirt upon reaching the goal on time, just relief that you made it by six p.m., avoiding emotional and financial stress. But take heart, for tomorrow you get to wake up and do this all again. Many single mothers live out this "six o'clock race" every day, not because they have considered all their options and deemed this the best one, but because childcare and work comprise the daily reality of their lives.

Beth, a computer analyst I met about fifteen years ago when she was newly single with a three-year-old boy, recounted her feelings:

> I had always enjoyed my work and excelled at my company. When my son was born, I took six months off and then worked part-time from home. The arrangement worked well. When the divorce came, suddenly I had to return to work full-time, and the search for good childcare was agonizing. Fortunately, my company was supportive and helped me get in touch with community resources that evaluate childcare centers and providers. Even with all this help, I felt anxious about my ability to work around the childcare provider's hours, and guilty about my lack of time with my child."

Beth is clearly in the "six o'clock race," and her comments highlight a number of factors about childcare that need to be discussed. Remember the old adage, "While we're making plans, life happens." That applies here. Beth had carefully planned her work life after her son was born, but now that she did not have the luxury of time, full-time childcare decisions needed to be made quickly.

I will never forget my own sudden return to work when my children were small. A friend kept them for me and I remember carrying the younger one in her pajamas and blanket, still asleep, to her house, the older one barely awake, dragging along behind. Gone in a flash were outings to story time at the library, as we all entered a new reality. My friend, Claire, (more about the role of friends later) was a lifesaver, but over the long haul, childcare requires a reliable, everyday solution. Whether you worked before your divorce or not, the new or increased demands of sole home responsibility will make you feel guilty about your children and your decreased time with them. Guilt is passed down from generation to generation in some cultures. I'm convinced that my own Irish relatives were able to put it in baby milk so everyone got their share. Instead of letting this consume you, don't wallow. Make a plan. Look for alternative periods of time to interact with your children and get creative.

Here are a few suggestions that have worked for me and other single mothers I've known with over the years:

Use travel time to talk to your children. We all spend considerable time stuck in traffic, whether driving, taking the bus, or on the subway. Take advantage of your captive audience and talk (cell phone, radio, and other technology off). Some of the best and deepest conversations I've had with my girls have been in the car. Tip number 1: Try not to drive off the road or fall off the bus if you hear something shocking. Tip number 2: Remember you're the adult and you're supposed to know this stuff; don't react. Tip number 3: If you drive car pool or ride the subway with your children and their friends, keep your mouth shut and you can learn about your children's social environment.

Remember Chapter Five, about home maintenance? Well, find ways to interact with your children as you take care of the house and prepare meals. Remember, the goal is to work together with your child, not land a page in *House Beautiful.*

Don't set aside a time when you decide to have an in-depth chat with your child and expect them to tell you their deepest fear in the thirty minutes you've set aside. Children are not alarm clocks. You need to look for those moments when they want to talk. Pay attention. Think about how you feel when someone close to you says, "Look, I've got fifteen minutes max, so fill me in on your life." If you resent that approach, so do children.

Since Mary Poppins is not available, you need to tackle the job of finding good childcare. The whole idea of finding good, reliable care can be overwhelming; there are childcare centers on every corner, home settings for care, and relatives. Even when you find them, what questions do you ask and what should you look for when you visit? What kind of care is appropriate for what age? All of this is enough to send you to bed with chocolate chip cookies. Fear not; help (and more cookies) is on the way.

A few general rules of thumb:

1. First of all, remember to trust your own instincts about your child and his or her environment (refer to Chapter Seven for reinforcement on this). If you enter a childcare center and the atmosphere doesn't feel right, then it probably isn't. Even if you can't put your finger on the problem, go with your intuition.
2. If your child seems agitated and upset on a regular basis with your childcare center, babysitter, or family member (yes that includes your mother), immediately re-evaluate that arrangement and look for another one.
3. It is always a good idea to show up at your child's childcare occasionally, when you're not expected. You can learn a lot. If you are ever told that you cannot come in for any reason, take your child home with you *that very minute*. You are the parent and people who care for your children are operating a business. You have a right to be there anytime.
4. Find out if your childcare center is licensed by the state. Call the state's Department of Human Services and find out where their office is and look up information about your child's center. You can see the file on the center which tells you a wealth of information

about teacher training, number of caregivers per child, and most importantly, background checks on childcare workers. The state also does regular inspections to see that safety features are in place, etc. You can see when the last inspection was done. This same licensing system is in place for in-home care, where a woman may care for children in her home.

In a number of states (my own Florida is unfortunately in this group), church-run childcare centers have been able to avoid state licensing by a law that allows them to take a religious exemption. What this means to you as the mother is that none of the information that I just discussed is available to you. You will only know what the childcare centers are willing to tell you. So, if childcare workers have no background checks, you have no way to know. There are church-operated childcare centers that are licensed, and those centers deserve credit for granting full disclosure and not hiding behind a religious exemption. Some unlicensed centers will tell you that they are accredited but not licensed. All kinds of accreditation can be purchased, but only the state can license and monitor your child's care on a regular basis.

To get the most up-to-date and practical information, I've turned to an old friend, Lenora Gregory, who has made a career in early childhood education and has directed childcare centers as well as being part of the planning for newly developing centers. Twenty years ago, Lenora and I, driven by our own struggle to work and parent, founded a non-profit organization called Family Care Connections to encourage and recognize the way businesses can develop family-friendly policies and programs, such as on-site childcare, flex time, back-up childcare, community resource information, and many more. For eighteen years, we have sponsored "Week of the Working Parent," which honors the top twenty-five family-friendly companies in our community. Eighteen years ago, we barely found five family-friendly businesses to honor. This year, we had to eliminate businesses to get it down to twenty-five! This was a good problem to have.

The following questions that I posed to Gregory were my questions years ago when I began the search for childcare, and they are still basically the same questions that mothers ask today.

The first and most important question that parents ask about childcare is, *How do I know that this is a safe, nurturing place for my child to be?* First, check and see if the childcare center is licensed in your state. Second, go observe the center for an hour or more; a few minutes will not give you a sense of things. Pay attention to whether you feel good being there or if it is a tense place. Third, ask any and all questions of the teacher regarding routine, discipline, curriculum, etc. Last, make sure you leave with complete financial information regarding cost, additional fees, and the rate you are charged for late pick-up. This can be high, so make sure you know about it up front. If you follow this routine with a couple of childcare centers in your desired area and price range, you will emerge with a center that is right for you and your child.

Now you are armed with some solid information to help you choose childcare. Selecting childcare for your child is one of the *most* important decisions you will make as mother. It is crucial to approach it as the mother-in-charge. If anyone tries to talk down to you with lines like, "Listen, dear, we know what's best for little Oscar. Just trust us," or "This is a church school that values children; you don't need to know more than that," leave that situation immediately. Abuse and neglect can occur anywhere, from family to church-run childcare. Be alert. If you have to hurt the feelings of a family member, friend, or church associate, so be it. The welfare of your child is the most important thing and *your* responsibility. Be the mother-in-charge.

Everyone knows that two-year-olds can't be left unattended, but the black hole of childcare is the age group of children called "middle school," from age eleven to fourteen. They are deemed too old for the Puddle Ducks Day Care, and they are the group of children labeled latchkey children. They are the ones who return home alone and let themselves in until parents arrive. Mothers worn out from paying for childcare and dealing with the routine often experience a sigh of relief when their child turns twelve and can, they feel, be left alone. In most states, twelve is the age that children can be legally left alone. Just because it's legal does not make it a good or safe option for your child.

As a school counselor, I talked to a number of children who were in this age range and went home alone after-school. Jay Jay was one of these children. He always hated his name because he said he felt like a rhyming page out of a Dr. Seuss book. He was twelve when he related this story to me.

"Every day, I take the bus home and walk two blocks to my house from where I get off," he said. "I walk slowly because no one is at home. I have to go inside and lock the door. It sucks 'cause other kids are out playing, but I'm not allowed. Mom says I should do my homework, but I just eat and watch TV; wish I could play." Jay Jay got home at three-thirty p.m. and his mother arrived at six-thirty p.m.

However, being bored and eating is the least of the problems that can occur. Patrick was thirteen, small with large glasses, and a serious student, but not "one of the cool guys," as he said, and desperate to be accepted. His experience was as follows:

"I walk five blocks home every day. Two of the cool guys walk the same way, but they always ignore me, or say things behind my back. A few times, I tried to talk to them but they just kicked dirt at me. I went in the house and did my homework. I couldn't believe it; one day, these cool guys started to talk to me, wanted to come in my house. Wow, I couldn't believe it was me they wanted to be me. Some other kids I didn't know came, too. They had cigarettes and pot. Said if I smoked it, I could be one of them in their club. I knew it was wrong, but it felt so good to be one of them."

Patrick got home at two-thirty p.m. His mother arrived at seven p.m. Both of these boys are at risk for problems because of the long hours they are alone. Both are basically good boys in difficult circumstances.

Jay Jay, who loves to play outside and is very social, feels trapped by his home confinement and was depressed and gaining weight from too many snacks. Patrick, on the other hand, lacking an outgoing nature and desperate to be accepted, even by classmates he knows are doing wrong things, is in real danger of drug involvement and possibly gang activity, since *club* is sometimes an early word for gang.

Over the course of the next two months, I spoke with both their mothers, and neither one had any idea how her son felt. Jay Jay's mother knew he was gaining weight, but she felt he was at least safe, locked in the house. Patrick's mother was pleased that Patrick seemed happier because he had new friends, even though he was vague about who they were.

While Puddle Ducks Daycare is no longer suitable, there are options for your child that you need to explore:

1. Check with your child's school and see if there are any after-school programs there.
2. Boy's and Girl's Clubs of America have after-school programs for this age that are excellent.
3. YMCAs across the country are the largest provider of childcare, for all ages, in the United States; the programs are of the highest quality.

The biggest problem in utilizing these programs is transportation, so talk to staff members. There may be a parent driving or a van from your child's school to these programs.

Look around your neighborhood and see if there is a neighbor who would let your child come there after school. You could pay them, or if they have children, you could take care of their children in return.

Over the last few years, people have become aware of how much at risk these latchkey children are. As a result, after-school programs are opening in many areas. Check with your local United Way for information about what's available in your area. Good after-school care is as important for this age group as it is for small children. The dangers are different, but every bit as real.

Childcare for my children involved all the options I've discussed. Their first experience was with my dear friend Claire, who helped me in the earliest days of my working. A wonderful woman named Mrs. Young kept them for a number of years as preschoolers, and then after school. Eventually, they went to after-school programs at their school. Friends continued to be a great support as early dismissal and teacher-planning days wreak havoc with the childcare routine.

And of course, there are no two more dreaded words for working single mother than, "I'm sick." Talk about upsetting the routine. It is an often-told family legend that my reaction to "I'm sick" was always to say, "Get dressed, you'll feel better." My girls quickly saw that it was better to get dressed and then throw up rather than argue with me about their condition. Sometimes, I even tried the other line, "You'll feel better when you get to school." This invariably did not work. I was buying time to figure out what to do, but I would not recommend this approach as a good strategy for handling sick children.

In my defense, feeble at best, in the years when my children were small, there was no corporate involvement in childcare as there is now, or family friendly policies in companies. In those days, women were afraid to say they were taking a day off to care for a sick child, but felt comfortable claiming car problems as a reason for their absence. Having used up a whole sick day for a parent conference or to see my daughter as an angel in a school play, I am astounded and thrilled to see companies allowing employees to take paid time off for the parent conference or the school play. It will always amaze me to go to an onsite childcare center at a corporation, such as Bank of America, and see employees taking their lunch hour in a small chair with their child at their onsite center. Some also have an onsite school. Many companies have leave days available for sick children and back-up care you can utilize if your child is ill or if your childcare provider does not show up.

When looking for a job, carefully review the companies (large and small) for their family-friendly policies. Women who work in these child-friendly environments would not leave their employer for lures of more money or other benefits. Their loyalty is where their children are considered an important part of their life. I believe that is a loyal, stable employee. Over the last fifteen years, I have kept up with my computer analyst friend, Beth, who was newly divorced with a three-year-old boy. Thomas is now eighteen and heading to college, and Beth, in a long-term relationship, has not remarried.

Her perspective today: "When I first got divorced, I was so worried that Thomas would grow up feeling neglected because I was gone so much. But it has worked out. When I wasn't working, we did things together. His friends were always welcome; on weekends, our house was the hangout. Finding good childcare for each age and stage was a struggle, but I found it and he was happy. He tells me now that he always felt loved and that I was there for him. I, on the other hand, feel I wasn't there enough. I think I like his version better."

Accept nothing less than the best childcare you can find, even if it takes a number of tries to get it right. If you get discouraged, think of Beth and Thomas.

To Become – A Detective Mother

1. Know all you can about your child's life – keep asking questions, listen to their answers, and observe their behavior.
2. 2. Be relentless about your child's childcare, and accept nothing less than a quality, licensed, and warm environment:
   a. Make after-school arrangements for your children ages eleven to fourteen, as they are at risk if left alone.
   b. Research companies in your area offering family-friendly work policies, then apply there for employment.

Chapter Eleven

Would You Like Me to Cut Your Meat? Family, Friends, Dating, and all that Stuff

In the year before my divorce, I met a couple with two children who had recently re-located to Florida from Minnesota, where I had lived and gone to college. New to Florida and missing Minnesota, we had a good time together discussing cultural and climatic differences (their snow shovel was quite out of place in the garage, and as for grits, I told them to think oatmeal with butter and sugar). In the process, we became friends. During the months surrounding my divorce, I did not think about the fact that I had not heard from them. Surviving the daily challenges of lawyers, children, and job interviews, and grappling with my own feelings left little energy to reach out to anyone.

When life settled down – normal as I knew it was gone forever, but settled was fine with me – I called my Minnesota friend to reconnect. She was cordial but not warm, and said she was sorry about my "unfortunate situation," a strange choice of words which reminded me of the way some southerners referred to the Civil War as "the recent unpleasantness." I guess the theory is that if you give something a gentle name, you can ignore the real nitty-gritty nature of the event. We made plans to meet in the park with our children, but that was cancelled, as were subsequent dates. I was concerned about what I might have done to offend her, but eventually gave up trying to connect. A lingering feeling remained that somehow I was at fault for the lost relationship.

About six months later, I ran into the only mutual friend that the Minnesota couple and I shared. I inquired about them and expressed concern that I had somehow offended them. I was not prepared in any way for my friend's response. She said that her husband and the husband of the Minnesota friend had become good friends and that he strongly discouraged his wife from seeing me because I was alone now and would be leading a much "different" life than his wife. He was correct, but not different in the way he meant. He also confided that he did not want his wife to get any "ideas" about being able to be on her own without him. Never mind that I didn't choose this state.

Apparently making the best of it was threatening. It is safe to assume from this conversation that, if I had fallen apart when my husband left and ignored my children's needs, then and only then, would it have been fine for his wife to be my friend. I recount this story because it was the first time that I realized that my divorce and how I handled it impacted other people and touched their own issues. The good news was that I could cross off my list the guilt for the loss of this friendship.

In my single parenting classes, I always shared this story because it opened up a whole area of thought and discussion, as new to the class as it was to me when it happened. It is important for your own mental health and well-being to understand other people's reaction to your divorce and their sometimes hurtful and baffling behavior. In order to help the class to read people better, we did an exercise that was quite revealing in this regard.

Recognizing that the divorce time is not your most self-assured, confident time, people close to us can be supportive, neutral, or destructive with their words and actions. I had the class keep a daily journal for a month of every interaction they had with people close to them. They were to record the interaction, what they talked about, and then (most importantly) record how they felt after these interactions. Talk about eye opening! Here a few of the class members and their experiences with the journal:

Marie, 34, Divorced Mother of Three

"At first I thought this journal idea was dumb, but I kind of got into it. My best friend is Rose. She's married, but her husband ignores her. I told her everything. When it was bad and I felt at rock bottom, she helped the kids and almost babied me. But as I read my journal, on the days that I got stronger and started to stand on my own feet, she always made me feel like I couldn't do it. I never saw her like this until I did the journal."

Marie discovered that her best friend really wanted to keep her weak so she could be the "in-control" person. Rose got a lot of positive feedback from being the caregiver and so she resented Marie's efforts to get her life together and move on. This was clearly about Rose's unresolved issues, not Marie's and her divorce. As hard as it is to accept, no matter how many bowls of mashed potatoes and chocolate chip cookies Rose brought Marie, a real friend encourages your steps toward mother-in-charge, not victim, and celebrates your success.

Jan, 28, Divorced Mother of One

"I like to write, so I didn't mind doing the journal, but I really didn't think this exercise would be of any value for me. There wasn't anything that I could learn about my friends and our relationships that I didn't already know. So it came as a complete surprise when I read my journal and realized how I felt after spending time with my childhood friend, Tom, who was gay. His life was about drama and he would call at all hours, involving me in complicated situations, requiring me to help, and then he pouted when I couldn't help immediately. In the past, I had always been available to him and enjoyed helping him. After we talked, I never felt like a good friend anymore. I always let him down. On top of that, our encounters let me feeling drained and depressed."

The reality is that when your life is relatively calm, you have sufficient emotional energy to deal with high maintenance friends. As Jan found out, when you are in crisis, you are using all your emotional energy to cope with your current daily life, not to mention the long range implications of your divorce. Jan came to realize she was not a failure as a friend, but in a crisis herself, needing to use her energy to survive. Since Jan was blaming herself and keeping it inside, Tom went right on demanding the same level of attention and resenting it when Jan didn't give it to him.

Merisa, 30, Separated Mother of Twins

"Since Tom and I separated, I could feel myself getting more and more depressed. He does not want a divorce and he thought having girlfriends was no big deal. He said I should be grateful to be supported well and ignore it. I was never real sure of myself, but I know how bad it made me feel when he came home after being with other girls. I thought of my whole life like that and I couldn't do it. Until I kept the journal, I didn't know how much my mother's daily visits were making me more depressed. She came every day to "check on me," as she said, and to see the boys. But when I read the journal, I saw how she told me over and over that given my lack of brains and abilities, how did I think I could manage and ever find another man. I should be grateful for him. Lots of women put up with girlfriends and so could I. It's hard to think much of yourself if your own mother doesn't think you're worth much."

I must admit that the class really reacted to Merisa's story and rushed in, all talking at once to try and encourage her own self-confidence. The sad truth is that nothing is harder for a woman than having a mother who is not your ally. For every woman who grows and flourishes in the unconditional love of their mother, there are many who have a lifetime of withheld love, unrelenting criticism, and jealousy. Merisa had became so used to her mother's criticism that she didn't realize until she read the journal that the main reason she was hesitating to divorce was that her mother was making her question what she knew she must do. Merisa's mother was a bitter woman and in a very unmotherly way wanted her daughter to share her misery. Maybe she was jealous of Merisa because she had the courage to end a situation that she could not.

For Marie, Jan, and Merisa, the experience of journal writing helped each of them see the relationships around them in a new way. It is never fun to discover that people aren't the friends you thought they were, but you are now armed with knowledge that can help you grow stronger and, perhaps along the way, more compassionate about the human failings of yourself and others.

For the next two months of the class, everyone followed (and yes, gave advice) to Marie, Jan, and Merisa about their relationships and how to handle them. Each of them realized that you don't need to end friendships or disown your mother, but there are ways you can change things. You are not a powerless victim. And this trio of classmates set about doing that.

Marie decided to spend less time with Rose while she was getting herself together. Marie identified other friends who were cheering her on to move forward and she realized that Rose's own needs prevented her from helping Marie in this regard. Marie maintained the friendship and only saw Rose when she was feeling upbeat, and then tried to focus in conversation on Rose's life. Only time would tell if the relationship could evolve into a relationship of equals, not a caretaker and dependent.

Jan realized she had always been open and honest with Tom, but she had not been in this case. She did not want to talk about the stress of her divorce because, somehow, talking about it made it all too real. Jan had Tom over and shared her feelings of being overwhelmed by her divorce and being scared to be alone and parent, and feeling like a failure as a friend to him. Tom had no idea about the depth of her distress, and because he cared for Jan, he started to be there for Jan. Of course, Tom pointed out that drama was just part of who he was, but he'd try to be less high maintenance. Once Jan was honest with Tom, the bond of friendship was strong enough to adapt to Jan's new needs.

It goes without saying that Merisa faced the hardest challenge of the three. Not very sure of herself to begin with, Merisa had a bullying husband and mother who were trying to control her behavior. She realized that she needed some help in dealing with the situation. First of all, she planned more activities with the twins, which prevented her mother's daily visits without creating a confrontation with her. Next she made an appointment with a counselor to work through her issues, and joined a babysitting co-op so her childcare was not dependent on her mother. The week the class ended, Merisa filed her divorce, continued counseling, and was on her way to taking responsibility for her life and children: a real mother-in-charge.

So far this chapter has been focused on understanding your friends and their reaction to *your* divorce. But it is extremely important to remember that you need to be conscious of being a friend to others, not just a recipient of your friends' help. Divorce is not a fatal or chronic disease requiring solicitous concern forever. "Victim women" try to make it that, but it's not. All friendships have times when one person is more in need of help than the other, but it is a balance of meeting mutual needs and, hopefully, long periods of time of calm and mutual enjoyment of each other. Remember how Merisa joined a babysitting co-op so she could attend counseling? The very nature of the co-op is that you help someone with childcare and then they help you. No money is exchanged, just mutual assistance. This arrangement allows you to share the give-and-take of a relationship, not just the take.

Often in my divorce and single parenting classes, people would say that they were so overwhelmed and lacking financial and emotional resources there was nothing they had to offer a friend. That is ridiculous and dangerously close to wallowing in self pity. Here are a few suggestions:

1. Take two minutes to call a friend and ask how they are and what's going on in their life. *Do not* discuss your situation.
2. Bake (or buy) some cookies or brownies and drop them off in appreciation of help received (driving your children, whatever it is).
3. Offer to keep friends' children for a night so they can go out and not pay for childcare.
4. Keep a list of friends' birthdays and send a card or note. It is always meaningful to have someone remember your special day.

Outside of expressing appreciation for friends' assistance, the best part of these things is that they make you think of other people and not just yourself. A large part of developing into a mature woman (the mature part does not mean that you wear ugly shoes) and a mother-in-charge is finding a balance between having a friend and being one. As Ralph Waldo Emerson wrote, "The only reward of virtue is virtue; the only way to have a friend is to be one."

For many of us in our mobile society – where school, jobs, relationships, and adventure take us far from the place when we grew up – friendships formed along the way take on the bonds of family. Author Jane Howard says it best in her wonderful book, *Families*,

> The trouble with the families many of us were born to is not that they are meddlesome ogres but that they are too far away. In emergencies we rush across continents, and if need be, oceans to their sides, as they do to ours. Maybe we even

> make a habit of seeing them once or twice a year, for the sheer pleasure of it. But blood ties seldom dictate our addresses. Our blood kin are often too remote to ease us from our Tuesdays to our Wednesdays. For this we must rely on our families of friends. If our relatives are not, do not wish to be, or for whatever reasons cannot be our friends, then by some complex alchemy we must transform our friends into our relatives. If blood and roots don't do the job, then we must look to water and branches.

Many single mothers who find themselves raising children far from home find that the friends they make become family as they share day-to-day life. Jane Howard is right; families will often go to great lengths and distances to be present in a crisis or for a major event. But what about all the things that don't rise to the level of a crisis or major event? People will travel great distances to be part of weddings, but a dance recital for a ten-year-old doesn't quite qualify. (It does for all of you who live with a ten-year-old ballerina, though.) This is where new friends become drawn into our lives and take on the role of family. You may be having a bad day and needing to talk, but you hesitate to call your mother three thousand miles away and unload on her, knowing she can't come to the door the next day to see if you're alright. The day-to-day is where we all live, in the celebration of a good report card for a struggling student or the trip to the emergency room with an ailing toddler. Friends: they all hold a place in our lives. Value them. Celebrate them and appreciate them. And don't be afraid to call them family.

No matter what your family or friends think of your divorce, most well intended but misguided people around you will encourage you to begin dating to "get over this" and find someone new. I have never understood the phrase "get over this." Somehow, it makes this life-changing event sound more like the flu or a bad cold than a divorce. Divorce, like any other major life event, gradually becomes part of your life and history as you come to terms with it. Most of this book is about how to do that in a way that makes you a stronger, deeper, and better person and parent. It is a gradual process. You don't just wake up one day, see a bright light, and declare, "I'm mother-in-charge."

The second problem with this approach is that finding someone "new" is not the answer. Someone new can be a person to go out with, enjoy, perhaps love or have a life with. But they are never the answer. The only answers are within yourself, as you evolve as a person. Many women quickly remarry, to recreate that sense of family. You do create a family, but as my Irish grandmother always said, "Be careful what you wish for."

When my second husband and I married, after being divorced for many years, we created a new family – complicated with different histories, traditions, experiences, losses, and expectations. Five children, eleven to twenty-three, two boys, three girls, comprised our household and in, case you are wondering, we did not resemble the *Brady Bunch* at all. I do admit, though, that on many a day I did wish that Alice would appear.

The one area of total, universal agreement in my classes was that after the trauma of divorce there was the trauma of dating.

What do most people think about when they think of dating?

- a nervous teenager asked out to the movies for the first time
- a high school senior nervous to come downstairs in her prom dress under the gaze of her parents and date
- sitting on the couch, holding hands, and watching a movie
- a bit older with your first apartment, getting dressed up for dinner with the cute guy in your office
- a first kiss under the tree by your house

- a four-year-old throwing up on your new black dress as you are about to leave the house (worse yet is if the four-year-old throws up on your date)
- an urgent call from the babysitter while you're at dinner that the pet gerbil has escaped and everyone is screaming
- a scowling teenage son, arms folded across his chest as you introduce your date
- playing "getting to know you" without discussing your ex-husband or asking for your date's astrological sign
- a potential romantic moment at the front door interrupted by the door flying open and small people (who should have been in bed hours ago) staring at you

Enough said. You get the picture, and if you're reading this book, you've lived it. All I can say is that dating any time after marriage is a challenge. The title of this chapter really is a true story from a friend who didn't date for four years after her divorce. With triplets, she was lucky to survive each day. A co-worker asked her out to dinner. She was so shocked she didn't know how to act, and almost reached over to cut his meat the way she did for her little ones every night. She definitely needed to get out more!

Here are a few thoughts about dating that I believe are important – wisdom gathered from friends, students, children, and my own experiences.

Never-Never-Never Date a Married Man

This was hopefully not an issue when you dated as a young girl, but it is now. I was shocked after my divorce to find that the married men I knew, often colleagues of my ex-husband or – horror of horrors – friends' husbands, asked me out. I was worried that I must be giving off the wrong signals or to blame for these approaches in some way. A close friend took me aside and pointed out that their behavior was related to their view of themselves and their lifestyle, not me. She was honest and direct. If I had been at fault, she would have been the first to say so. Big relief, but it made me very cautious with anyone married.

You need to commit this next part to memory. It does not matter if a married man tells you that:

1. he is unhappy and misunderstood
2. he has a marriage in name only
3. he hasn't had sex with his wife in "years"
4. he's separated
5. his wife has a terminal disease and has three weeks to live
6. he is about to be separated
7. divorce is final next week

He is still married. In this area, you must set hard and fast rules for your own self-respect and respect for the institution of marriage. If he is so misunderstood, ignored, with no sex life for ten years (although there is that awkward matter of a five-year-old to explain), then he can face up to the crumbling, non-existent, sexless marriage he portrays to you, get a divorce, and then date freely. Don't compromise here. Remember, even if he looks and acts like the love of your life, he is someone else's husband and he is disrespecting his wife. You don't need to be the next woman he disrespects. Anyway, be positive. There are good single men.

Don't Feel Pressured to Date

One day in class, the subject of dating came up (as it did a lot) and one of the most positive and talkative women in the group, Angela (forty, with two teenage boys) said that after her divorce, all her family and friends pressured her to date because, as we previously discussed, that was a sign to them that she was "over it" and moving on. Translated, that meant they did not need to worry about her anymore! After a lively class discussion,

Angela realized that she really didn't want to date, but did feel pressured. Remember, your life is not about doing what others expect or need, but what you expect of yourself and need. Listen to your own heart and trust your feelings.

Don't Share Your Personal Life with Your Children

Mother-in-charge is always mother, not roommate or buddy, and your home is not a sorority house. You are entitled to a personal life. No matter what your children may say, no child really wants to know the details of your relationships. But children always need to know where you are and how to reach you. As children grow, they will expect and desire privacy for their personal lives; grant yourself the same.

Don't Act Like a Teenager When You Start to Date

One of the themes that emerged in the children divorce group was their general discomfort about how "weird" mom got when she went out on a date. Children are used to moms having friends – male and female – but even though they couldn't explain it very well, they were unsettled about how mom acted when going on a date. Teenage children were equally unsettled, but far more articulate about the situation.

John, age sixteen, was the older brother of one of the students in my divorce group (Tim, age eight). John helped out in the after-school program with the children and that is how I got to know him. He mentioned that his mother had started dating again, and I asked him how he felt about it. He was very adamant in his response:

> I like for my mom to go out and be with men who treat her nice, but I hate the way she acts before a date. She gets all giggly and silly, fussing over her clothes and taking forever

> with make-up. She's supposed to act like a mom, not like a teenager.

John hit upon a truth which is at the root of a lot of dating issues for divorced moms. Teenagers are just coming into their own, trying to be grown-up, worrying about their looks, feeling awkward with the opposite sex. It is very scary for them to see mom – their security – dressing and acting like a teenager over a date. Never underestimate how important it is for you to be mother-in-charge, helping your children through the awkward teenage years, not competing with them. Date like the adult you are now, not the teenager that you used to be.

Do Respect Your Home as a Safe Haven for Your Family

For children, home is their world, where they know what's in the refrigerator, where the cookies are kept, where they hide stuff that nobody's supposed to find – and where they can be completely safe. Never bring anyone into your home who does not respect you or your children and their safe haven. If you follow this rule, all the questions about *what if* and *what should* will answer themselves.

From our parents and siblings, who anchor us to the past, and our grandchildren who rush past us into the future, and all the people we meet along the way, possibly love, maybe marry, hopefully befriend, make up our lifelong journey of family – divorce is a transfer station on the journey. As Leslie H. Farber sums it up:

> The family is inescapable. You may revile it, renounce it, reject it . . . but you cannot resign from it. You are born into it, and it lives with you and through you to the end of your days. Not only that, but its memory will prompt you to fashion new families, of blood or water, either in its image or – just as telling – quite unlike it. Nobody goes for long without some

semblance of a family. If we lack a conventional one, we are certain to grope, ingeniously or awkwardly, for a replacement. We confer the status and importance of relatives on the people at the office, at school, down the block, in the platoon, or wherever else we may find them.

To Become – A Gracious Woman Who Gives and Accepts Friendship

1. Remember that real friends encourage you to succeed and never put you down.
2. Be the friend that you want to have.
3. Date only when you are ready and date like the adult you are and not the teenager you used to be.
4. Celebrate and cherish the friends you meet who become "family."

Chapter Twelve

The Person You've Become: Random Notes and Thoughts

A couple of years ago, I was giving a seminar on work-family issues and someone in the audience asked me how I thought my divorce and single parent years had changed me as a person. While my exact response eludes me today, the question is one that has remained. In Anita Shreve's novel, *A Wedding in December,* old high school friends meet twenty-seven years later to celebrate the wedding of two of their own who had been high school sweethearts, lost each other, and now were marrying. One of the characters addresses this very issue when he says, "But only one life could be experienced. The other had to be imagined." Since I cannot picture any other me who made different life choices, I would have to say that the mother-in-charge role thrust upon me at thirty caused the growing-up process to accelerate. I was no longer part of a marriage, two people committed to each other and their children living out a life. I was "it" and had to work through my own issues to become mother-in-charge to my girls.

Some people reading this book are probably wondering why I haven't discussed the role of your former spouse in raising your children, strategies to make it easier, etc. The reality is that everyone's situation is different. A close friend who divorced with three sons was held close by her ex-husband and his family and they are a tremendous support. Another friend with twin girls has never heard from her ex-husband in thirty years. Neither have the girls.

No matter what your former spouse does or does not do in terms of parenting, you need to become mother-in-charge because the only person whose parenting and life you control is your *own*. Be the best person and parent that you can be, and don't try to control anyone or anything else. Support and help are wonderful beyond measure, but even without it, you can do just fine once you decide to be (tired of the phase?) mother -in-charge.

People in my divorce classes were always asking:

"Will it all work out?"

"Will my children ever recover emotionally?"

"Will I ever be happy again?"

"Will I ever have another relationship?"

In order to answer some of these questions, I have contacted a number of women friends to help you look forward in time and get a glimpse of how it all turned out for them. Most have been divorced at least ten years. All have children, and two divorced after long marriages. A couple are re-married, with step-children.

1. Looking back on your years as a single mother, what is one piece of advice that you would give a young single mother today?

Jan: *First of all, avoid being a single mother if you can! Not by giving in all the time or by sacrificing yourself to stay married at any cost or by enduring abuse of any kind, but rather by being discerning in the choice of a mate and by being equipped to live as a whole person, inside a marriage or outside. But, if you are in the role of single mother, avail yourself of all the support systems you can muster, be honest with yourself and your children, and use your strengths to become a good example and a role model for those children.*

Meg: *Please remember not to use your children as pawns in the relationship. Children should have the freedom to love their father. In their own time, they will understand.*

Claire: *Take time for yourself. Get a babysitter or have someone watch the kid(s) at least once a week so you have time to remind yourself who you are and to do the things you're interested in. Even if you just go to a movie, you need the break. If the only thing you have in your life is your kids, then you don't have anything to offer them.*

Jennifer: *I think I would say, don't hate. Negative energy might serve a purpose at first, but after that initial period, to hate an ex is like you're drinking poison and hoping the ex will die.*

2. Did being a single mother change you as a person? If so, how?

Jan: *Absolutely. I was married until my children were teenagers, so I never had issues of childcare, custody, and so on. But I did have serious economic issues and major emotional issues. I had to overcome my hurt and humiliation and fear because I owed my three daughters the knowledge that a woman can survive and even prevail in this world. I was largely content as a stay-at-home wife and mother, and I was good at that position. Starting over as head of the household and breadwinner was a monumental challenge. I don't know how I would have done it if I had not had to be an example for my daughters. With the help of good friends and family, I was able to work toward a stable career, home ownership, financial freedom of a sort, and prove to myself and to my children that it could be done.*

Meg: *I believe it did change me. I was able to focus strictly on what I felt was in the best interest of the children. My confidence returned after years of being told I was incompetent, etc. My personality was freed, I could re-establish childhood friendships, show my children there were wonderful relationships built on respect and love.*

Claire: *I became a much more patient person. I also think that being a parent, in general, is a very introspective process. As a single parent, it's even more pronounced. You see and hear so much of yourself coming back at you in the look, words, and tone of voice of your kids. I learned a lot about myself – especially in the early years – that helped me to be a better parent in the long run.*

Jennifer: *Being single made me more industrious and creative. I didn't get child support, so I started freelance writing to make ends meet. Now, I have been published in over forty magazines. I wanted to improve my home but didn't have money, so I went to the junior college and took plumbing, electricity, and carpentry. I would have never had these experiences if I had remained married.*

3. Do you think your children would have been different if you had remained married to their father? If so, how?

Jan: *This is hard to say, since they were well on their way to adulthood when we divorced. However, I do believe that they chose their mates on a much more mature level that I did, and that they play much more equal roles in their marriages today. I think they are better wives and mothers than I, in many ways, and their children have more involved, loving fathers who have a respect for their wives and homes and families. Confidence and communication play a major role in this.*

Meg: *I would have to believe the children would be different. We walked on eggs for so many years, probably not realizing the full extent of the controlling situation we were in. Fun and laughter returned. Open communication became the norm. Fear retreated from discussions on difficult issues.*

Claire: *Yes, I do think my daughter would have been different if we had remained married. In some ways, it's easier to be a single parent. There are no mixed messages. There's more consistency and she always knew (except when I surprised her) the way I would react in certain situations. We lived a very contented, peaceful life together. It would have been much more erratic if I had remained with her father.*

Jennifer: *I think they would have a different picture of women. Now they expect women to be equal partners. Perhaps they would have different expectations if they had seen me as Tom's "little woman."*

4. Do you feel that you are in a good place about yourself today?

Jan: *I am. I am financially stable and secure, although far from rich. I don't need to be rich. I'm close to being ready to retire and I am looking forward to that. I wish I had a man in my life, but I'm not afraid of life without one. And, I would never settle for just anyone in order not to be alone.*

Meg: *I love my life today. While not as financially secure, I am so much happier. No more tears. Free to be me, as they say. I'm enjoying a wonderful relationship with my children, their husbands, and my grandchildren.*

Claire: *Absolutely! I successfully raised a terrific kid who grew up to be an exceptional young woman. I have loved being her parent more than anything I've ever done. It is the thing about which I am the most proud. And it was the most important work I'll ever do.*

Jennifer: *Yes, I have touched the bottom and it was FIRM. Today I have an interesting life running a business and pursuing my lifelong dream of organic farming.*

5. Any other thoughts or comments?

Meg: *It's such a cliché to say time really heals, but I truly believe that statement.*

Claire: *I never set out to be a single parent. But when it happened, I did what I had to do to make sure I could make a life for me and my daughter.*

Looking back now that she's grown, I can't imagine my life any other way. She can't, either. I used to worry that perhaps she needed a more "normal" family. But the fact of the matter is that she was a better-adjusted young child than most of her friends who lived in two-parent households. I guess I feel that it doesn't matter whether you're raising a child alone or with a spouse or partner. Being a good parent is what matters most. As long as you take a thoughtful approach to the job, things work out for everyone.

Jennifer: *Avoid thinking of your life as a soap opera segment. Life really is what happens while we are planning otherwise. Each choice changes everything. We are not victims unless we allow ourselves to become victims.*

Including the perspectives of these women was important to me because when I was a new single mother, I did not know one divorced woman in my situation, and insights like these would have been helpful to me, as I hope they are to you. Their experiences are definitely food for thought, especially on those rainy, dark nights when you're prone to stress.

A common thread with these women, and all of the women that I talked about in this book, comes down to one word: believe. In yourself and in your children.

Remember Tinker Bell in *Peter Pan*? She carried a small packet of fairy dust to sprinkle on people to give them belief in magic, and it worked very well in convincing Wendy and her brothers to fly to Neverland with Peter. Wendy was fairly practical, so until Tinker Bell came along with fairy dust, flying would not have been an option. This book has been about increasing your level of fairy dust so you can become mother-in-charge and believe in your ability to be that. But, it is not enough to stop there. You need to believe in yourself and a future for you, full of possibility beyond your single parent years. Your children will grow up and the mother-in-charge needs to move to the next phase of life. All your good work in raising your precious children will be damaged if you unreasonably hang on to them as they start their own lives. Get busy with your life, and as inspiration, I suggest you read a very special book about the wonderful surprises life can bring when we're no longer young and may be lacking in sufficient fairy dust. *A Thousand Days in Venice* by Marlena De Blasi, the true story of an American woman who begins a whole new life and relationship when she least expects it. If Marlena's book does not point you toward the many possibilities of the future, then sprinkled fairy dust is not enough. You need a transfusion of the glittery stuff.

Recently, I heard Jack Welch, the former CEO of General Electric and business guru, speak. He is short and wiry and full of energy. A member of the audience asked him where he got his incredible self-confidence, which was apparent in his presentation. He said that he was an only child of Irish parents and his mother told him every day that he was six foot four and brilliant – and he believed her. Every child needs that one person (more than one is great, but one will do nicely) who believes in them, never gives up, or lets go. Author Kenneth Keniston once wrote, "Every child needs to grow up with one person hooked on him." It is that unconditional love that has no limits or qualifiers, but does have expectations which grow out of your incredible belief in the potential of that child. It is the single most powerful thing you can give a child: your passionate belief in them and the promise that you will always be there for them. There will be missteps and lost moments, but over the long haul, you're there.

I have a friend who is a pediatrician to my grandchildren and he continues in the footsteps of my wonderful pediatrician, J.K. David. When I went to talk to Dr. Steve Lazoff about single mothers and what advice he would have for them, he spoke of the magic of childhood and the need for young children to view their parents, for the first ten years of life, as super-heroes who will protect them. They need to feel that way about both parents so, as we discussed in previous chapters, do not demonize your former spouse, because the only person you are hurting is your child. In the magical thinking process of the child, those larger-than-life parents will protect them from being abandoned, and should protect them from the harsh realities of life. He did not speak about what age to abandon a pacifier or introduce solid food, but about a style of being a mother that conveys caring and consistency. In his view the other details, the pacifier or solid food, are really details the significance of which is overshadowed by the bigger picture which is the secure, loving environment that you create for your child.

Suffice it to say that no child goes to first grade clutching a jar of baby food and sporting a pacifier around their neck, and if they did, their classmates would handle it. One of my brothers sucked his thumb for as long as I can remember. He liked to accompany thumb sucking with rocking back and forth, not necessarily in a rocking chair. Any chair would do. This made our cross-country car trips as children quite entertaining. Personally, it made me seasick. As a child psychiatrist, my father, after a few attempts to break the thumb sucking, let it go and decided he'd give it up when he was ready, or the first day of school, whichever came first. He contended that peer pressure eliminates lots of behavior that parents can't. Sure enough, the very first time he put his thumb in his mouth and his classmates laughed, he was done. In case you're wondering about his teeth, he never had braces.

"Dr. Steve" as the children call him, really believes in the magic of his young patients and their mothers. Keep looking for your J.K. or Dr. Steve. They do exist. I've been lucky enough to have two of them in my life.

There are some events which seem minor when they occur, but over time reveal their significance. "The Dollhouse Adventure," as I like to call it, was one such event. After I had been divorced about three years, I decided that we should get a dollhouse and work on it together. I already could envision this dollhouse handed down to the grandchildren, a lovely, beautiful treasure. On a trip to the local toy store, the perfect dollhouse was found. It was a bit disconcerting, though, that the dollhouse came unassembled, but I was reassured by the cheerful storeowner: "It was easy to assemble and I did it in an evening." That is a quote because, to this day, I still remember those words, and was haunted by them for a long time.

As you can imagine, I had the girls all excited about the dollhouse. So on a Friday night, we had pizza (as was our routine) and settled down to "build our house" so to speak. I was shocked at how many pieces were involved once we emptied the box, and even more dismayed by the complex directions. The thought did cross my mind that perhaps the directions for assembling a nuclear warhead had found their way into the dollhouse box. While assembling things was not my forte, even I was discouraged that beyond direction A, I was lost. It became clear after more pizza that, despite the encouraging words of the toy storeowner, this dollhouse would not be ready for furnishing tonight. We were all disappointed and went to bed. Over the next few months, I tried again, but to no avail.

At the school where I was a counselor, I had been seeing two special needs children who were siblings, for about a year, and had gotten to know the family well. The father was a carpenter and he heard about the dollhouse that wasn't and said he wanted to do something to thank me for my help with his family. Now the house would be assembled by a real carpenter. The girls helped me put the box in the car as we waved it off on the next leg of its journey. About a week later, the carpenter/parent reported back that the dollhouse was assembled, but he had to abandon the directions because they were inaccurate. (See, they *were* directions for a nuclear warhead.) Whether he was truthful about the directions or he was trying to make me feel better, I'll never know. It was probably a combination.

What a glorious day when the dollhouse returned home, enthusiastically welcomed by the three of us, as my fantasies about the antique dollhouse passed down for generations of granddaughters and great granddaughters re-emerged. The dollhouse was a source of fun for us for many years, but not in the way that I envisioned. We did not create an heirloom, but we had a wonderful time painting and re-painting rooms, wall papering, collecting fabric scraps from home decoration stores, and finding small furniture and, of course, a suitable family. Yes, this family did have a dog. Rooms had dotted and spotted walls; some rooms had all four walls of different colors, very *avant-garde*. The house was decorated for Christmas with tiny trees and gifts; a reindeer even got stuck in the chimney. What was emerging was a wonderful, fun-filled project, but nothing that would survive to be handed down to anyone. At some point along the way, I understood that this dollhouse was not about the future, but about the here and now, the pleasure the girls got in re-decorating or painting. At one point, they took great pleasure in having the front of the house pink and the back white. In the grown-up world that they would soon inhabit, that kind of creative decorating would be frowned on by the neighbors. But my children's imagination knew no bounds, or color, in our dollhouse world. It finally came to me that we were building memories that would outlast any antique, never decorated or loved dollhouse.

And the memories have lasted and a new generation of little girls and dollhouses is emerging in our family. Last Christmas, Laura, in Spain, wanted a dollhouse for three-year-old Sophie. Thanks to Pottery Barn Kids, a fully-assembled dollhouse traveled overseas to the delight of Sophie. Last week, Barbara and I were in a store with two-year-old Holland, and a wonderful, already assembled (operative word) dollhouse caught my daughter's eye. Soon the furniture saved from the dollhouse of old will again come to life, for precious Sophie and Holland.

This book was not about perfection in ourselves, our children, or others (even dollhouses), but about fierce devotion to becoming the best woman you can be and a mother-in-charge. It is about the fierce devotion to your child and his or her healthy and happy development, no matter what it takes to make that happen.

In my mind's eye, part of me will always see Barbara and Laura as those little girls crowded around the pumpkins or peering into the dollhouse. But there is another picture of them there, too. My husband and I were together at the beach last year and it was a moment of pure joy for me to see my daughters, caring, nurturing young women, tending to their babies; Sophie, Max, Eva, Brantley and Holland, and Harrison, supported by their good husbands, laughing together.

So, armed with chocolate chip cookies for the bad days and fairy dust to remind you of the magic, go forth and raise your children, build your life, and never lose sight of the incredible, endless possibilities that life has to offer.

To Become – The Best Woman You Can Be

1. The only person you can control or change is yourself – repeat this as often as needed.
2. As you evolve into mother-in-charge, you give yourself confidence and your children security.
3. Your child needs you to believe in him, never give up on him, or let him go from your life.
4. Always believe in the endless possibilities in life for you and your children.

Acknowledgments

To all the women who, over the years, have shared their life stories with me as they assumed the role of single mother and moved away from an often dearly held marriage, into new realities and unexpected joys. To the children who, with their honest words, direct gaze, and open hearts, gave me insight into their fears, misconceptions, desires, and keen observations about their parents' divorce and their place in their newly formed families. Knowing them all has made me a better person.